Data @ Risk

by
David Stelzl

Dave Stelzl

Data @ Risk

Published by Bravado Publishing
www.bravadopublishing.com

ISBN 978-0-9821755-5-2

Printed in the United States of America

Acknowledgments

Writing a book is always a challenge. It's exciting when you begin, then as things progress and get refined, it becomes difficult. I appreciate those who have spurred me on to continue the effort and to get it done. First I would like to thank my family who constantly puts up with the rigors of my travel and speaking schedule. My wife and seven children – some who help out a great deal in the office, making it possible for me to even take on a task such as this, and those who are younger and putting up with less of my time. For my wife who ends up carrying the load for homeschooling, running the house, and all kinds of unexpected emergencies that seem to come up when I travel. And for my children who have encouraged me for years to illustrate my own book, which I've finally done in this latest work.

Before publishing I always ask for people to read my drafts providing input, counsel and critique. In particular I would like to thank my editor Kristen Bailey, who has put in many hours reviewing my changes and challenging me to write clear concise, readable text. And Lynn Bowen who frequently coaches me on my writing and provides a great deal of input the mechanics of good writing. I am also grateful for the help and insights I've gained from Henry Stelzl, Jim Guido, Michael Santarcangelo, Jay Haller, Bill Sieglein, Bret Straffon, Chris Thatcher, and many of my friends at the National Speakers Association who have provided a great deal of encouragement as I write and speak.

Author's Note

Security is a discipline – a process some call it. I call it a discipline because it is something that has to be developed in the culture and in the mindset of each employee, whether an asset owner, asset creator, user, or administrator. This writing represents my perspective based on working with many companies across the US over the past 10 years and some internationally. While this is not a technology book, some attack methods have been named here and will likely change. Regardless, the concepts are still real and will likely be relevant for years to come....

Thank you for reading, for attending conferences and events I have spoken at, and for providing input that has both allowed me to improve my message as well as clarify it for non-technical audiences. My goal is to make this simple so that we can all get involved.

Take the mindsets – begin a program to build awareness in your company, and keep it going. Continue to read, to understand, and to assess. Partner with companies that specialize in assessing and helping companies of your size and vertical.

Table of Contents

Part One

Dave Stelzl

Introduction

In my seminars, I ask, "When was the last time you experienced a major security breach, including a company wide virus outbreak?"

The typical response is zero. Not us. Yet every day I read a news article detailing how another company was breached – social security numbers exposed or credit card numbers stolen. The reason companies feel safe is these breaches often do not disrupt the company's computer system.

The reality is we need to change the way we secure data; we need to change the company culture to ensure that the intellectual capital your company profits from is safe. You promised customers you would keep their information secure and private, so you need to ensure that information really is safe.

Companies need to create an *asset mindset,* and I'll explain how to do that.

People probably know what physical assets their company has, what products they offer and what markets they serve. They also know about hackers, but they don't understand the growing volume and importance of digital assets, and what underground organizations have discovered: how to profit from your company *without disrupting your business*, and often without anyone noticing something is wrong.

Security product companies love technology and make claims of impenetrable products that will ensure safe computing. They claim their products are secure but they love to speak in a secret language of protocol stacks and packets. Outside security experts further confuse things by using terms like polymorphic and misspelled words such as phreak and toolz. It's a secret language of three letter acronyms, shortened words or code words such as bot and spear phishing. There is a sense of control as they watch over organizations' IT departments and build an empire around the data center, promising to keep all data from the hands of illegal proprietors.

An uncaring security professional may joke at the expense of "end-users" who know little about the on goings and internals of "EBCDIC and ASCII code," or who cannot find their way through the complex mazes of the registry. These end-users secretly access material online, all the while being watched electronically by unauthorized big brothers who read their email and advertise discreet chat sessions to those who sniff network lines in their boredom.

"quick, here comes the boss - get out the
techno-geek phrase generator"

Most security initiatives are led by technologists who understand the hacker's methods. Yet the people who create and own these corporate assets have no real understanding of what type of risk they are up against. While technologists are guarding the castle, they are unaware of changes in data value that come with business climate changes, pending lawsuits and advancements in product development discoveries.

Employees have taken the data with them on the road, to their personal email accounts at home, and have stored them on portable media, personal computing devices, and in unsecure email programs for all to see. The information is hacked. Then a day comes a few years down the road that one of those hackers makes a mistake. Perhaps it is an information buyer carelessly using fraudulent credit cards, and the operation is blown. But it's too late to stop or fix the problem, because customers have been exposed and years of secrecy unveiled, exposing the company's latest achievements to the competition.

Let me reassure you now, this book is not about technology. Instead it's written to those who own and use digital assets. This book is about building an asset mindset that understands and handles these critical assets with great care. This kind of asset is ubiquitous, yet it requires extreme confidentiality. It's so valuable yet weighs nothing, is relatively invisible, and is easily stolen because it is never displaced, but simply copied.

Part One of this book explains what is really happening to digital assets, who is behind it and why, despite the increasing investments (approaching 12% of the average information technology budget) we're still seeing exponential increases in data theft. This type of theft has grown from nothing to over $1 trillion dollars in revenue over the past few years, up from $67.2 billion just three years ago.

Yes, there is a lot of hype out there, and security product companies want you to buy their silver bullet. So in Part One we discover what the real problem is – and it's not a technical problem. We'll lay the foundation for changing a mindset that has hurt us for the last decade. The old mindset says data is safe behind the corporate firewall. But after reading Part One, you will have a completely new way of explaining what the problem is and evaluating the efficacy of your company's defense without getting technical.

Part Two presents seven critical mindsets that must permeate the thinking of those who own digital assets on the business side: the people with liability and those who use digital assets. You'll be offered a new way of thinking about digital asset protection and given new ways of working with information security professionals.

If you happen to be a security professional, you'll be given insight into the roles that corporate leaders should be playing in this present warfare. We also offer ideas on how to present complex security concepts to those who may have shown little interest in the past, and have not understood how to properly discern risk levels and investment needs.

Finally, in Part Three, we discuss how to secure your assets, the role of technology in creating a secure computing environment, strategies that different software developers and technology companies have taken and the effectiveness. You'll learn how to change the overall security culture in your organization to help increase the privacy, integrity, and availability of the information your company depends on as you compete in a global economy that faces the threat of very sophisticated thieves.

Things have to change if we are going to continue expanding our networks, mobilizing our work force, and providing universal access to our data.

Chapter 1

A New and Better Mindset

How should corporate managers think about security and risk?

Corporate leaders need to protect the organization's most critical assets; delegating this responsibility to network and system administrators, without executive involvement, is no longer an option. In fact, companies that continue to treat digital asset protection entirely as a technical issue will face significant losses, liability and disaster. Why? This kind of target has become a major source of fraud and economic growth for those who make a living preying on the unaware.

Early in my technology career, I managed the distributed computing area for a highly recognized national bank, and my job encompassed all local and wide area networking, file servers, non-mainframe servers, databases, and applications and desktops.

One Friday afternoon a frantic manager and a line of dark suits formed at the entrance of my cubicle. Apparently some application was down that handled our wire transfer system. They insisted my team report to a building across the street where this particular file server was located. This server was installed and managed by the local department that handled wire transfers and not located in the data center where most servers resided. It sat in a tangled mess of

Token Ring Type 1 cable (something from the past), out of the way under a work table, and then connected to workstations throughout the office.

My team members and I looked at each other with the same question. "What exactly is a wire transfer system?" No one knew, but someone thought it had to do with transferring money between accounts.

We were all frustrated at this point, but for different reasons. To the managers this seemed like a matter of life and death to get this system back into production. My frustration on the other hand had to do with the hour. It was five o'clock and I was going to be late for dinner if I didn't leave soon. In fact, my entire team had the same problem. We had no concept of why this application meant anything to our company. To us, this was a hardware issue with the server.

Do you see it yet? This is the technology mindset verse the asset mindset. Management was looking at an application that was malfunctioning and therefore not generating money for the company. This asset was no longer an asset. On the other hand, my team was looking at the technology and wondering what component might be bad and where we might get a replacement. It was not part of our thinking that this was costing the company money – it really didn't affect us in any measurable way. So why couldn't it wait until morning. It was clear at this point that my management role did not have much weight compared to the executives waiting on us. No one knew to build an asset mindset into the thinking of my support team, and we were all paying for it at this late hour.

Budgets are established for three reasons: growing the business, reducing risks associated with the business, or creating operational efficiencies. When money is spent on technology, it's because someone on the business side of the company determined that a new application will further the business, reduce risk, or increase operational efficiencies. Infrastructure is purchased to support the new applications, usually when someone from the Information Technology (IT) area has determined that the plant and equipment (in this case the networks and servers) will no longer support the increased load.

Then, after the fact, technology administrators may prompt the organization for new security devices based on threats they've personally seen or experienced, or more likely because technology sales people prompted them. Security budgets are based on felt pressures by both government regulations and IT. Justification will be made by pointing to unmet government requirements, suspected intrusions, or in response to an outright attack on the company; the latter being the least likely.

Since 2003 we have seen a decrease in harassment type attacks such as web defacement or crippling virus programs. In some ways it's tempting to think that threats have diminished, except for the alarming number of cyberthefts being reported in our daily newspapers. These cyberthieves hide themselves so the few attacks that are discovered don't trigger enough of an alarm to demand action.

By 2000, brute force hacking and stealing passwords became the crime of the day. Codes infected systems and destroyed hard drives after presenting the end user with a message of peril. Hackers refocused on viruses that could wipe out an entire company in a matter of seconds, or create such havoc that companies were forced to shut servers down and disconnect PCs from their network. Advancements in such malware enabled programmers to develop "worms" that would spread virus-laden code universally before antivirus signatures could be deployed. Some of the more advanced variants reported covering the entire Internet globally in as little as eleven seconds.

An alarming saturation of malicious code threatened corporations world-wide with nothing to stop the viruses save technology advancements. The response was anti-virus software and more emphasis on patching systems. Finally, zero day response was announced as the silver bullet every company needed. Companies including ISS, Entercept, Black-Ice and Okena were battling for the number one spot in zero-day defense at the desktop as well as inline technologies that would thwart these malware worms before they reached the server or workstations.

Compared to current day exploits, the zero-day, purely technological, approach neglected the core issues that define risk and remediation. That approach left corporate asset owners out of the picture and even thought that math and encryption would cure all information security woes. But this is far from true as we can see today, despite some very significant advancements in security technology.

The motivations behind early attacks show why technology took the approach it did. Web defacement attacks were the first attempts to prove one could travel across the Internet and break into a company unnoticed; it provided a sense of accomplishment for clever computer geeks who were challenged to break through popular firewall technologies. When administrators finally gave up, hackers counted it a victory.

When it comes to risk, there are two questions asset owners should be asking: what is the impact, and what is the likelihood? Companies need to look at the data, the digital assets companies create and use in the form of intellectual capital and customer information as an example. Since around 2003, cybercrime has taken on a new face, and now more than half a decade later, the goal is no longer notoriety or political posturing, but rather a generation of greed. Dishonest financial gain capitalizes on the flawed security architectures present in most companies today.

We are no longer dealing with computer geeks but savvy criminals.

When I hear managers talking about budgets and security, I know they are caught in the technology trap. This is what I say – If the risk is real, managers must get serious and start reallocating their budgets. I have been working to change the technology mindset and educate business leaders on digital asset protection by providing a simple explanation of how security works, where companies have gone wrong, where technology fits, and how to move your corporation toward a state of digital asset protection.

I worked for McNeil Consumer Products, makers of Tylenol, when they were attacked by criminals putting cyanide in their capsules. I've traveled nationally and internationally working on security solutions to protect against some of today's greatest threats to corporate data. From this experience, it is my belief that we have allowed this discipline of information security to become a black hole. No one outside of the technical IT organization can understand all this and take action. It's been made into a complex technical problem. Every day, companies are asked to spend millions on more security products without having an overall plan that actually improves the security strategy. I say, let's get our money's worth if we're going to spend the money. Let's spend it on the right things – the things that will really bring an increase in the overall security of your company's digital assets.

Bad security decisions lead to losses in data, personal liability, and even business failure. People who design inadequate security likely don't understand how security works, or how to combine various aspects of a security system to secure corporate assets. They instead create a complex, technological masterpiece that appears to provide new levels of security but often a false sense of security. Then, when the system is breached, they wonder what happened, or worse, marvel at the technology used to attack a company's core assets.

This is why asset owners, those who own data along with its associated liability, must get involved. Those who use the data must change their mindset in order to reduce exposure to corporate assets. Those who administer and manage systems, applications and associated data, need to see the asset perspective on securing data if they are to help executives make wise technology decisions. I will provide ideas to accomplish these goals and to communicate truth to business leaders, enjoining them in making wise decisions concerning security budgets and technology choices.

Technology should bring greater functionality to an organization, and security can sometimes inhibit this. As Bruce Schneier writes in his book *Beyond Fear,* security is really a trade-off, trying to determine where risks demand restrictions, and where the likelihood of an event is so low that it doesn't warrant restrictive security measures. If we think of security in business terms, we'll make better decisions that place fewer restrictions on the business units that need data and accessibility in today's competitive market.

First - Redefine Security as a Discipline

Many companies put information security under technology. Other groups might handle supporting infrastructure disciplines such as telecom, storage management, enterprise systems, application development and network support. With this structure in place, technology experts are asked to build information security programs across the other disciplines within a fixed budget. This centralization of security decisions, without adequate understanding of the business units and applications they are supporting, leads to "bolt on" security technologies. These often provide less security than originally desired while crippling business operations. Overall, an ineffective and unacceptable security strategy emerges.

Further exasperating this situation, third party technology manufacturers and integrators operate in ignorance of the root problem. They operate under the notion that security is mostly a technology problem, a strategic error that leads to bad security. Infrastructure offerings such as Voice over IP (or unified communications), enterprise servers, application development and software have encouraged technology integrators to treat security as just another product when, in fact, it is not; security is a discipline. It is a discipline that involves protecting corporate assets (digital assets); something that cannot effectively be added to an existing technology infrastructure.

Making Security Part of the System

Let's assume you're going to buy a car. Would you purchase one without security or safety features, and then hire an auto company to add the security controls?

This might have worked for information security before security became a part of the core infrastructure. While automobiles have many add-on features, their basic structure includes safer design, security glass and meticulous engine placement to reduce injuries in head-on collisions. These security features aren't treated as post-sale add-ons. In fact, many consumers consider security to be their top priority when shopping for a car; just ask any Volvo owner.

Security is a discipline that must be applied to core products in the technology sector as well. Cisco and Microsoft are working hard to build security into their products. It's not hard to visualize every router and switch having firewall, intrusion detection, spam filtering and anti-virus software built into the network. Instead of installing several different products to stop viruses, spyware and spam, they could simply be part of the operating system. Just look at the marketing behind Vista, and Windows 7, Microsoft's latest operating system. Regardless of whether the technology actually does what it claims, the marketing behind it is strong because the concept does make sense.

In the storage world, EMC outperforms all other providers, with twice the market share of its closest competitor, IBM. What is EMC selling? You may be thinking the obvious, storage. Or perhaps you know this company a bit more intimately and you answer, "software." But actually, the answer is security. You see, they know who holds the assets. They know that you are depending on them to house all of the data your company uses, and so they have slowly morphed their message into one that speaks about asset security. They offer access control, reporting on who accesses data and when and even maintaining the integrity of archived email. Security is built into the storage process.

Let's take this thinking a step farther. Is it wise to build an entire application without first considering security? You cannot add safety features to cars after building them. You simply can't add enough safety designs post production to keep someone alive in a head-on collision or high speed crash. Computer systems should work the same way; designed with security *built in.*

This is also true for phone systems, networks and applications, although additional security can be required later on. The technical industry has somehow convinced asset owners that we can add information security to our systems as an afterthought. Most of the best practice thinking comes from influential marketing hype.

Making Security Part of the Culture

But technology alone, even with security built into the system, won't secure assets. The people are an even bigger part of the issue. Without a safe driver, a car manufacturer's safety design is powerless.

Every person in your organization that touches technology must understand digital assets, whether they are the owner, the user or the administrator. Careful handling of data comes from the top down and must be defined through the procedures that a company or division puts in place to guard these assets. We will address this in more detail later in the book, but at this point please understand that security is more of a people problem than anything else. One article I read stated, "Get rid of the people, and you will get rid of the security problem." Of course we can't do that, so we will have to look at other alternatives. But one could argue that the more data users you have in your company, the less secure you will be. Data users represent the largest hole in the security equation, so developing a security-savvy culture will go a long way in protecting your data.

The Truth about Security Budgets

Over the last six years, IDC studies show steady spending increases in security hardware, software and services. Forty-eight percent of this money is spent on services, thirty-three percent on software and nineteen percent on hardware.

As I write this book, 11.4 percent of the average U.S. IT budget (according to IDC) is allocated for security projects, with most of the money used for policy and procedure changes. This number will grow over the next few years as cybercrime threats escalate.

Eleven percent is a significant amount when you consider the total IT budget, but it's important to understand that security money is being spent in almost all corporate divisions—not just the IT departments, so it's actually higher than the 11.4% I quoted. Yet, no matter how much time and money companies spend, cybertheft reports continue to grow. Even while you're spending more, the problem is getting worse. It seems like a no win situation.

Part of the problem stems from the "disconnect" between those creating the budget and those responsible for spending it. The complexities of security technology, rapid change, and foreign language have evolved so that corporate executives can't understand or manage this growing budget. Managers hand this money to information security groups or IT to solve the problem, and then assume everything is secure.

IT teams are destined for failure when this happens because they lack the important understanding of what they are actually securing: the value and relevant corporate threats to the data. IT sets out to secure the network when managers want the data guarded. These two things are not the same.

Consider a recent example in Europe where an employee placed media containing highly sensitive personnel information in the interoffice mail. The package was misplaced or taken, exposing millions of dollars (or the Euro equivalent) of information to possibly the wrong people. The Wall Street Journal reported on this mishap, posing the question, "If this had been in the form of money, would the owner of this data have given this to someone to mail without any level of security or tracking method?" The answer of course is no. Why is money so protected, but not data? The answer, "Simply because those working with it rarely understand its value." I call this the *technology mindset*. A mindset that takes care of the network and systems as a technologist would care for a machine.

There is a lot of money being spent on security, but it is not well spent. The budget might not need to grow, but it needs better direction. <u>Only asset owners can initially know and understand the value of their data, and it is their job to understand how to protect it and how to educate those who will touch it.</u> When given this understanding, they are able to delegate the care of this asset where physical, technical and administrative controls will help to ensure its safety. Both must come together, the *technology mindset* with the *asset mindset*.

Two Principles of Guarding Corporate Assets

Stop focusing on technology and focus on the assets. Know who the asset owner is and let them drive the level of security required for any given asset. These are the two key principles that would, if taken seriously, change the way we protect data today.

When one focuses on the technology, the technical team takes complete responsibility without having any true liability. Yet, the asset is used and controlled by the business issues and decision makers—those with the liability and ultimate responsibility. Intellectual capital, writes author Mack Hanan, is the only margin sustaining aspect of your business. The concept of digital asset value is one of an asset mindset which must be given to technologists along with adequate funding. This funding will be based on information collected by both asset owners and technologists and is addressed later in this book.

Asset Owners and Technologists

The ultimate understanding of asset value, along with the real liability, rests with the asset owner. This is generally a business person who has responsibility for the business and controls who uses this data. Digital assets include customer information, intellectual property of the business, trade secrets, account numbers and financial data. The asset owner must be involved whenever security is considered.

Data users create and use data while those responsible for IT support functions are tasked with managing and securing it. Both must have an asset mindset. The technologist will actually have both mindsets. Security is increased when these two groups take on the mindset of an asset owner, even before money is spent. While they will never hold the same level of liability, they do play a significant role in determining the asset's level of risk. Data users, the ones who create the greatest exposure, can play one of the most important roles in maintaining an adequate level of security.

It is the asset owner's job to help data users and technologists develop the responsible mindset of data ownership. This requires an intimate understanding of data value and relevant threats (something I will cover later in Part One).

This book will help asset owners, data users and technologists and IT managers. All three will play a key role in changing the trends we are seeing today in information theft. Bear in mind, only the asset owner has serious liability, and therefore must take this responsibility seriously.

This book explains security and the asset mindset in simple terms that can be applied by asset owners. It will help foster an asset mindset with those that create, oversee and use data, and for those who must justify more relevant steps to securing data.

The Role of Technology

When it comes to securing data I find that data owners are confused about the true threat to data and the role technology plays in making data secure. Data administrators also are misinformed as to the true impact of compromised data and associated liability, and they may misunderstand the changing threats associated with business climate changes.

In the typical security meeting, technical people lead the discussion while asset owners are half listening with the false assumption that it will be handled. The discussion turns technical: "We need to harden this, lock down that, close off these ports, layer security, replace our firewall technology with another, turn on event correlation or network time protocol, and possibly add some type of IPS that will feed into our SIM. All this depends on having some type of ESM which should connect with the ITIL initiative which is built on the newly installed CMDB."

Lost? So are many others. Once this starts, data owners turn on their Blackberrys looking for their next meeting. Can you blame them?

When an intrusion does occur, it's considered a technical problem. The problem is, security is not really a technical problem. It's a people problem, and more often than not, the problem at hand could have been prevented if some data-user's mistake had been avoided, or if people using or managing this data had really understood its value.

With the mistreatment of technology and the abdication of responsibility to secure assets, I believe that most companies today have a major flaw in the underlying strategy they use to secure these assets. Throwing more money at this problem won't reduce the risk but it will cost your company a fortune, and possibly your entire business.

A New Mindset

Threats are changing, and the big issue is controlling digital assets. Technology, user awareness and careful handling of the data can work together to increase the level of protection given to any digital asset.

Minor philosophical changes in the way you approach security can greatly increase the effectiveness of your plan. But in the end, three mindsets must change:

1. Asset owners must take on the responsibility for making sure digital assets under their jurisdiction are secure. This means helping data users understand the value of the asset and knowing who should and who should not have access to it. It means helping data administrators understand the asset they are working to protect. Asset owners will be required to stay involved in the security planning to ensure data is secure over the life cycle of the data asset.

2. Data users must understand the value of the assets they are using, how they are exposed through daily work habits, and how the threat landscape changes with the business and as new scams are constantly developed by cybercriminals. They will need to know what activities increase the risk of data loss such as misuse, and theft. They should understand threat levels as risk changes with data age, company activities, competition and even the internal people threats.

3. Data administrators must develop an asset owner mindset, taking time to learn about value and risk associated with the assets placed under their stewardship. A technical mindset is sure to end with data compromise and misuse if not combined with the asset mindset.

Throughout this book I offer simple models and examples of data assets and security measures that will help data owners understand where to get involved and where to delegate. You'll learn why data security is currently failing and how to turn the tide.

Data administrators can reposition yourselves, not as an obstacle to business progress, but an enabler who can help data owners understand security in their terms so you can get the right budgets approved for the right initiatives. In the end you should be positioned as more valuable to the organization and better able to align IT with the business. First, let's take a look at what is really happening in the computer crime world.

Chapter 2

The Real Threats

Will your current data security strategy thwart the new breed of attackers?

As quickly as computer technology changes, the motivation and techniques of cybercrime follow. What was once a malicious high-schooler demonstrating newly learned scripting techniques is now a world of crime potentially more powerful than illegal drug trade.

Every company with important data has a major security concern, even if they fail to see malicious activity. Understanding this can mean the difference between a "safe feeling" and an effective security program. Don't be fooled by smooth running systems and implementations sporting the latest antivirus and intrusion detection software. Security is not just about technology.

Identity theft hit home for me in 2003 when I had the opportunity to travel to South Africa on business. With no time for sightseeing, I grabbed souvenirs at the airport for my wife and children after a short two day meeting. This was the only purchase I placed on my personal credit card.

About 20 hours later, upon arriving home, my wife greeted me at the door and informed me the bank had called repeatedly, requesting a return call as soon as possible. They would not tell her what the issue was, but indicated it was urgent.

"Mr. Stelzl, have you been in South Africa recently?" a representative asked when I returned the call. It seemed odd for the bank to know this, but I answered affirmatively.

"Did you purchase a large quantity of hydraulic equipment, in an amount approaching $25,000?" he asked. "We have a record that someone made a card-present transaction of that amount just yesterday."

This meant someone in South Africa had actually presented a card with my name on it to a merchant and made a purchase. It was frightening to discover that someone at the airport had taken my card number and turned it into a credit card.

This incident occurred at the beginning of the credit card-fraud and identity-theft trend that has lasted nearly half a decade and was expected to grow by 15 to 20 times based on reports from *USA Today* in 2007 – We have certainly seen this happen. At the time, I didn't understand how easy it was to duplicate a card, but today we hear about it almost daily.

So, how does this happen?

While scaring you with crazy stories may be entertaining, it's not all that effective in helping you fix the problem. So I'll give you a clear understanding of the security risks and how you can manage them in your business. Understanding where these attacks come from will help build a foundation for creating an asset mindset throughout your organization. In the end, security needs to be a part of the culture as you create and use digital assets.

The Changing Faces of CyberCrime

In the October 2004 issue of *SC* magazine, Ron Condon of Gartner describes the new world of hacking. The original hacker, he notes, was the "spotty 14-year-old who just wants to show off to his friends." The new world is composed of attackers—many from Eastern Europe or Russia—whose goal is much more sophisticated than the thrill of breaking in. "These people are in it for the money," Condon writes. *Network Computing* magazine reported in January 2007 that credit card and social security information can sell for as much as ten dollars apiece through identity-thieve controlled internet websites similar to EBay.

About twelve computers in an average organization encounter some form of malicious program in any given week, according to CyberTrust (recently acquired by Verizon Business), a firm dedicated to security consulting and managed services. About six sexually explicit graphics will be exchanged, and there's a 65% likelihood that a breach will involve someone on the inside.

These statistics highlight visible security problems, but they are not necessarily the most damaging. Companies would like to eliminate them, but are often unwilling to spend more money than already allotted. In many cases, viruses have been handled adequately through antivirus applications with regular updates. Spam is seen as a nuisance that is being reduced by filtering. And so it seems, your security problems are few.

Since my trip to South Africa, credit card fraud has accelerated, and identity theft has become the fastest-growing crime in America (and accelerating world-wide). The problem has escalated to information theft of many varieties. Yet many of these activities are not evident until it's too late.

Examples Close to Home

In June 2004, Brian Salcedo, age 20, pleaded guilty to four counts of wire fraud and unauthorized access to a computer after he and accomplices Adam Botbyl and Paul Timmins used an unsecured wireless network at a Lowe's store in Southfield, Michigan, to steal credit card numbers. Salcedo and his friends first stumbled across the network the year before, when driving around town and using their laptops to locate wireless Internet connections (a practice known as "war-driving"). Upon finding the Lowe's network, they hatched an idea.

Working out of Botbyl's Pontiac Grand Prix, the group planned to access key systems and "skim" each card swipe from stores around the country, including California, Florida, South Dakota, Kentucky, North Carolina and Kansas. They downloaded and modified Lowe's custom software that processes credit card transactions, known internally as tcp credit, creating an almost undetectable tool for "skimming" card transactions. This was an obvious move away from the traditional hacking through firewalls to deface websites or to shut down systems. They were not out for notoriety but rather financial gain.

"Whoops - Crashed the Point of Sale System"

On November 5, 2003, Salcedo and his pals used a common Trojan program, readily available online, to gain access to Lowe's credit card transactions. Their modified tcp credit program was unsuccessful at first, but they managed to "crash" several point-of-sale systems at the local store. These system failures alerted the

Lowe's IT department to investigate, and they notified the FBI of suspicious activities.

Two days later, an FBI surveillance team observed Brian and an accomplice using laptops and two suspicious antennas mounted on their automobile, which sat in the parking lot. This time, the hackers' attempts to install the modified tcp credit software were successful, and they began to skim credit card information as each purchase was made.

Later that evening, FBI agents could pinpoint what was happening by reviewing Lowe's log files at its North Carolina data center. Only six credit card numbers were actually stolen that night, but if Lowe's had failed to recognize that something suspicious was occurring, every customer might have been forced to order new credit cards. More importantly, merchants and banks all over the country might have incurred the expenses associated with fraudulent charges and card reissuance. Laws passed over the past few years would now require Lowes to notify all past customers of the breech, which is helpful to the customer but bad for the brand.

This attack was pulled off by a couple of amateurs with the type of training provided to the average network administrator. This wasn't even a professional that knew what he was looking for at first; it took this group months before they realized the money-making potential. The damage caused by these amateurs, however, was significant.

Salcedo's actions could have resulted in up to $2.5 million in damages (according to Lowes' reports), and he was sentenced to nine years in prison. But an even greater problem will continue to haunt Lowes: its reputation.

One of Salcedo's accomplices moved on to became a security consultant, as many apprehended hackers do. A word of caution here: hiring people involved in past cybercrime theft may bring talent and insight found nowhere else, but I don't recommend it.

Use people trained to secure things, not people who have damaged others.

So what's the unique aspect of this story? They were caught.

Not an Isolated Incident

Shortly after the Lowes incident Citigroup had to notify 3.9 million customers that computer tapes containing their personal data were lost while en route to a credit bureau. CardSystems Solutions, a company few had heard of before June 2005, was breeched, exposing more than 40 million credit card numbers. The hackers used a "skimming" program similar to Brian Salcedo's.

At the same time, *Secure Enterprise* magazine listed additional attacks, including unauthorized access to systems at ChoicePoint, DSW Shoes, LexisNexis, Polo Ralph Lauren and several universities, including Carnegie Mellon, Boston College, Tufts and two Universities of California campuses. The list goes on. Ameritrade, Bank of America and Time Warner also reported losing data on tapes, exposing sensitive customer information like credit card numbers, social security numbers and other information that could be used to create fraudulent credit.

The Identity Theft Resource Center posted the names of nearly 140 companies that reported ID theft in 2005, with 57 million exposed customers. By the end of 2006, this number had reached almost 200 with nearly 100 million exposed customers.

By 2007, this list grew to 303 companies including very large banks, universities, and a large number of government organizations housing a great deal of personal information; 2008 numbers have now exceeded 600 companies. The number of compromised identities, including one of the largest heists ever with TJX, was now at nearly 200 million, *or almost two-thirds of the US population.* (Note: recent attacks against Heartland may prove to exceed the losses of TJX.) In the case of TJX, members of an organized crime ring had actually set up accounts on internal systems, posing as employees. They used Trojan programs installed between the point of sale systems and processing systems to skim data over a period of three years. They were finally arrested when outsiders purchased the stolen data and were caught buying gift cards at Wal-Mart valued around thirty thousand dollars. To date, nine individuals have been arrested in connection with the TJX crimes and are in the process of being sentenced.

To see how true the numbers are, I frequently poll audiences when I speak and find that over half of any given audience has in fact had credit cards and account numbers compromised. Some individuals suffered severe forms of ID theft, involving lawyers and bad debts.

I also ask how many attendees have had a major security issue in the past year of virus outbreaks or web attacks. The number is always low, measuring in the 1% range. My polls, although unscientific still show that virus attacks and web defacements have been replaced by money making schemes including information theft and resale, espionage, and some instances of extortion. This corroborates reports I am reading in the news and other industry related periodicals.

Many of the companies experiencing these crimes (as reported in IDTheftCenter.com) have well-planned security strategies, 24/7 monitoring systems, intrusion detection programs and other safeguards. Through my work, I know that they have made significant investments in securing data. Yet, these companies continue to experience loss. If data is unsafe with such large and well equipped organizations— some of which are required to comply with federal regulations like the Gramm-Leach-Bliley Act —how can smaller organizations with limited IT budgets claim to have security "covered"?

With the available data, no company or individual should feel secure with our present systems and methods of dealing with cybercrime. Instead, we need to be on alert and proactive.

Your Call to Action

As a data owner, your job is to understand how security crises occur and educate both your data users and those responsible for securing it. I mean this from a business perspective. In other words, only you (the data owner) can really know how this data can be used on the black market, or who would want to steal this data. Only you know the true value of it to your organization and what it might mean to someone else, such as your competition or investors. This means you must be observant, taking into account who is likely to misuse corporate data and where attacks might be initiated. You should also know who internally uses this data, where and how they use it, and where insecurities in the procedures and applications might exist. As I mentioned up front, there will be trade-offs in between productivity and security here, and only the asset owner is in a position to make that call.

Who is behind these attacks?

Understanding Organized Crime

Imagine what it would take to move tons of illegal substances (drugs) into our country through shipping, customs and the logistics of warehousing. After that, drug traffickers have to sell the product and keep a very visible activity undercover. There are major expenses involved.

Now consider how much easier it is to simply hire a technical person to use the Internet to break into a large retailer's database. There aren't warehouses, ships, planes or customs to deal with. The data is stolen, copied to disks you control, and distributed anonymously through electronic media via the Internet. Money exchanges hands electronically; it's all very clean, and all very profitable.

Over the past couple of years Dateline has run at least two specials on this topic, showing us just how easy this is when they sold a credit card number online for eight dollars. It took these novice reporters just 30 seconds to make the sale, and as they watched online, they were able to track spending all around the globe just seconds later. Now multiply this by thousands or millions. All of the sudden, this eight dollars can turn into some real money.

It should be no surprise that organized crime is involved here. John Sileo, author of *Stolen Lives*, shared with me in a recent interview just how "organized" organized crime is getting.

USA Today reported this to be a US $67.2 billion business in 2006. In 2007 McAfee CEO David DeWalt shared with us that cybercrime had become a $105 billion business. Today we have FBI reports that state revenues from stolen information are exceeding the one trillion dollar mark.

For the first time, cybercrime has surpassed the value of the illegal drug trade worldwide. Back in 2005, *USA Today* reported that cybercrime was expected to grow more than twenty times in the coming three to four years. We are actually seeing his happen with exponential growth that seems to have no end.

Cybercriminals are running a company just like you do, with the exception that their business is illegal. Still they have employees, benefits, pay plans, co-workers, managers and staff and even subcontractors. And you can be sure there is an R&D department working on new techniques to steal assets, as well as new ploys to turn data into money.

Recent reports track major growth coming out of China. Former military intelligence analyst Scott Henderson tells us that Chinese hackers form the largest hacker presence world-wide, and these hackers aren't hiding. They maintain an open web presence and some even run hardware and software advertisements on their hacker websites, which may indicate some level of funding. CRN reported that one in three Chinese middle schoolers are studying to become a hacker when they grow up. It's the cool thing to do – a rock star kind of status. In all there are close to 300,000 known Chinese hackers, forming somewhere close to 250 different cybercrime organizations. Some of these organizations employ tens of thousands of people specializing in everything from software development to the selling of stolen information.

Insiders

Information Week recently conducted a poll of corporate IT employees and found that 100% of respondents have their resume posted on the Internet. The poll found employees will leave when offered a 20% raise in pay.

This means that every IT department has many resumes posted online which describe the company's IT environment, important applications, location, the operating systems and even the patch levels you have your systems at today. But there is more to this problem. These resumes also advertise the people who are inside and who might be willing to take more money if the opportunity presented itself. So while I am not saying that all IT people would compromise their ethics for money and give up company data, I am saying that there are those out there who would.

Organized crime members need a way to gain access to your company and will look for an IT person or data user, with a resume posted online, who is somewhat disgruntled with the company. Perhaps this person doesn't like their manager, didn't get a recent promotion, or it might be something as simple as not getting an office that recently opened up. Now they are mad at the company and perhaps willing to do something unethical if the price is right.

The manager of the organized crime company contacts them anonymously through the Internet, offering to pay three or four times their current salary in exchange for some help. None of this involves breaking and entering, murder, or even vandalism. In fact, the punishment for this type of crime is often far less than the penalties for physically stealing from a convenience store (although laws are starting to change finally). So they take the offer, the money is exchanged online anonymously and the task is performed. It may be looking the other way or it could involve inserting a memory stick into certain servers, while not even knowing what is actually happening. The point is, it's a very simple and easy task for a lot of money, and it's very hard for the employer to detect. We may never know who was involved.

This may be why so many intrusions involve insiders. The person on the inside isn't usually masterminding these attacks; they are simply a subcontractor who might not even see the overall damage. It is important to know who is handling data, and to put controls in place much like those used in accounting to stop fraud.

Who's Vulnerable?

It's no surprise that banks and card-processing companies like CardSystems are targets, but universities are also at great risk. According to *USA Today,* students are prime targets for information theft because they have a limited credit history, take out loans, sign up for new credit cards and often forget to pay bills on time.

While data analysis reveals more than 200 million identities were exposed by 2008, studies reveal far less of this data actually being used by criminals What accounts for the discrepancy?

The hackers behind these crimes often keep a low profile and take more information than they immediately use. Suspicious activity may show up on consumer accounts months or even years after a security breach, so people must monitor their statements and credit history. In fact, professionals are not likely to use your credit card numbers for purchases, but rather to establish new credit cards and loans that will take much longer for victims to discover. These provide a much greater revenue potential for the con artist.

When I served as director of security for a global consulting firm, I received call after call from security product manufacturers who wanted me to carry their product lines. Armed with the latest data, they were ready to show that companies could have been immune to attacks of the Code Red Worm, Slammer, Blaster and others if their products had been on board. It was tempting to remind them that if companies had simply kept their Microsoft patches up to date, this would have prevented worms from spreading.

Hackers and their techniques are a moving target. Understanding how the landscape is changing, and who is behind the attacks, offer clues to defending corporate systems. Corporate managers are frequently unaware of attack sources.

In the Lowe's case, the attack was opportunistic. Salcedo's friends claim they were merely looking for an email access point when they stumbled upon the Lowe's network. This may or may not be true, but they likely did not intend to steal credit cards when they first discovered the network. I'd guess they were initially just trying to gain access to various corporate networks for the fun of it.

Today's hackers have an ever-increasing bag of tricks for cyber-breaking and entering, and they're in high demand around the world for their industry expertise. In 2006, the *Wall Street Journal* ran a front-page story about a businessman who hired hackers to extort a company for refusing to do business with him. This practice has become common throughout the world, holding an online company hostage in demand for some sort of pay out, with a promise to start protecting them in the future from similar threats.

With the growth of cybercrime and the sophistication of attack methods, these organizations are expanding their reach, targeting the small to mid-sized businesses which tend to be easy targets with less security in place.

Beware of Spam

Organized crime is also responsible for building large spam relay services to market everything from Viagra to hardcore pornography. Don't be deceived; spam, while it is clogging up the Internet, may also be carrying something much more alarming. Spear phishing is an attack method using attachments and links that look legitimate. They may be legal documents, forms, or news reports specific to a person's job in your organization. Once opened, these attachments may actually look real, but are infected and sent from an illegitimate source. The virus infects the system with code that will track future passwords, emails, or find data asked for by the attacker.

A recent example reported in the Wall Street Journal told of a group that sent out thousands of subpoenas to corporate CEOs. The email appeared to be a pending law suit with a link that would allow the receiving CEO to view the legal document. Once clicked, a "reader" was downloaded and the CEO was presented with the legal document. The subpoena looked real. Meanwhile, code was being installed on the receiver's PC. Over two thousand CEOs admitted to clicking the link and believing the email was real. These computers needed reformatting; notice that the antivirus programs were ineffective in this case.

Searching the Net

As websites get more sophisticated, cyberthieves are finding new ways to compromise them. The problem with security is that programmers are always looking for new functionality, not greater security. Security is a reaction. Often we develop something only to find that it has created another security problem. One such discovery was made as Google JavaScript programs were compromised this past year.

Most are aware that a Google search will bring up both good and bad sites for a given topic. Some of us actually have anti-virus programs that will flag infected sites, note that others are untested, and put a green symbol by those which are safe to click on. A recent attack changed all of this. This attack surreptitiously compromised links so that the user, after running the search, was presented with the normal links, but when clicking on them would be infected by malicious code. The user was still directed to the intended website, and therefore unaware that anything was wrong. However the program loaded onto the computer enabled a hacker to gain access to their system using some type of Trojan program. The infected computer may then be used to spam others or the hacker might begin collecting passwords to the databases and applications your computer is used to access.

In this case, any website that Google indexes could be suspect if it does not handle JavaScript correctly or securely (JavaScript is responsible for many of the cool features including changing colors when you mouse over objects). Some of the sites affected included Wired, CNET, TV.com, USATODAY.com, ZDNet Asia, History.com, and many universities. This was a single incident, but seeing this type of attack will allow others to copy it. Security groups will likely respond with some type of patch or fix that will solve the immediate problem, only to be followed by some polymorphic copycat, meaning the attack can be changed to disguise it from automated security safeguards such as antivirus products.

In summary, expect more attacks to come through targeted email and legitimate web sites that have been compromised. While these sites don't remain infected, hackers can install their password stealing code long enough to capture thousands of transactions before being discovered. Over time this adds up.

Attacks are Well Planned and Highly Successful

Hacking is big business for organizations that need money and aren't concerned with staying legal.

Organized cybercrime is a relatively recent phenomenon, according to John Lyons of the United Kingdom's National Hi-Tech Crime Unit (NHTCU). "Three years ago, there was no sign of organized crime...this has only come to light in the past 12 months (Written in 2004)," he writes. Organized crime members are developing relationships with hackers who will work for cheap rates for groups like ShadowCrew, an early cybergang responsible for significant acts of information theft. Lyons says Russian programmers can earn 10 times the going commercial rate by switching to illegal cyber-activities, including credit card fraud, extortion, spam and even distribution of pedophilia materials.

What are these groups really after? The October 12, 2006 edition of *USA Today* exposed the real story behind organized crime. Organizations who steal this data are making a fortune operating in online chat rooms, compromising databases and stealing their information.

It would be foolish for us to think this is just another virus. This is a business looking to control a lot of information with a strong financial return. There is money to be made using data that's generally easy to obtain. Using technology, social engineering and the cooperation of disgruntled employees or strategically placed hired criminals, hacker organizations gain access to some of the most valuable resources within a corporation.

Hired Guns

Another common ploy is using extortion or revenge to make money. As reported by the Wall Street Journal, Businessman Jay Echouafni hired hackers to use a network of zombies to blackmail a Florida firm because a business deal didn't go the way he had planned. Using a process called distributed denial of service attack (described earlier), these hackers were instructed to attack the target company's site, taking down its web server—a critical part of daily business. Echouafni demanded a large sum of money to stop the attacks, which had caused about $200,000 in lost sales and system damage. By aiming a botnet, consisting of hundreds of thousands of compromised computers (zombies) at the target, Echouafni's hired attackers made hundreds of thousands of requests against a single web server, a task most web servers are not equipped to handle. The overtaxed server is taken down by overload.

SC magazine reports more than 250,000 new zombies are created by hackers each day to carry out large-scale attacks. Over seven million zombie computers form large scale botnets around the world, and in fact, seventy percent of all spam emails are sent through these networks.

Imagine a worldwide network of zombies ready to launch a focused attack on a single entity, flooding it with so many requests that it crashes. The well documented Storm Network is a great example of large scale botnets. Comprised of reportedly millions of systems, this botnet has the power to do tremendous damage to almost any corporation.

Where Are These Zombies?

If you're wondering where all of these zombies are hiding, they're likely in your company, on some of your most powerful systems, computers, laptops, teleworker computers and perhaps even your personal computer. In 2006 a study released by Microsoft revealed that an estimated 60% of all systems outside the corporate network contained botcode that my result in that computer being part of a botnet. The 2008 FBI crime report showed we are over 90% infected today. Chances approach 100% that your network hosts zombie infected computers. But don't expect to see them at work. Hackers go to great lengths to keep these infections out of sight and operational.

The Power of Social Engineering

Perhaps the most powerful method of hacking into your data comes from a non-technical source: social engineering. While IT organizations are reviewing the latest in firewall technology, intrusion detection, and anti-malware devices, the real thieves are conning their way through a complex web of deception. Social engineering is a key reason why networks and systems cannot be secured against cybertheft.

In 1995, Check Point introduced a stateful inspection firewall that supposedly covered all layers of the network and application. It was impenetrable in the eyes of many. While technology companies have leapfrogged each other in this area of security for years, arguing whose firewall is harder to defeat, the real thieves have been talking with administrative assistants, call center operators and front line data users, gathering all the data they need to set up authenticated connections to your company's most prized possessions. So while these advancements in firewall protection are important, social engineering goes on unaffected by these advancements.

Security really is a people problem, and many experts believe that security technology is largely there to stop rookies, not professionals.

Consider your data users. Just about everyone in today's corporate world has access to data, and it is often the less likely targets that create the biggest problem. People don't think that email addresses, employee ID numbers and even branch addresses are secret. Perhaps, by themselves, they are not. But when someone calls the receptionist asking for engineering and is able to get a name, access to your web, your branch locations and general managers, that person begins building the tools and language needed to convince insiders that they are also an insider.

On the weekend, in the middle of a road-closing snow storm, they are on the line with IT, pretending to be that person from engineering, needing access to an application. They know the general manager's name, they have the office location and they become Bill Smith from engineering. They need access to the application to complete a project for their boss, Andy Thompson. They have Bill's ID number from the administrative people, but they need access to the VPN. They may not have a password, but that's ok. They call another branch person, acting as an IT person to trouble shoot an access problem. By talking that person through the download of a patch, they install a remote access program on the target system, gaining access to the network. This isn't very complicated, it's just a well formed ruse using insider information and lingo they have picked up by talking with various people in the organization and perhaps some online reading. It's not hard, yet it is nearly unstoppable. Technology alone will not stop this attack.

Who is the target? Often people not in the IT group and not related to computer security. It's the data users. People, who naturally trust the system, have a job to do and want to help out their fellow workers. When IT calls, they are cooperative and anxious to get back to work. Protected by standard security technology, your organization is defenseless against this attack.

What Are They After?

Today's cyber-criminals are after three things: money, information that can be sold for a profit, and computer resources. All, in the end, focus on some kind of financial gain.

The purpose of identity theft is to generate money by using names to apply for loans or create credit cards and other forms of credit. Pretexting, or pretending to be someone you are not, is a powerful ruse used to apply for new credit cards, loans or other sources of borrowed money. In the past year, organizations farming identity data have multiplied, commoditizing the price per record. Higher end organizations have focused more heavily on company secrets and other forms of information that command a higher dollar value.

Computers are needed to carry out these lucrative crimes. Hackers may use zombies to infiltrate target systems. Linking these together, hackers then form large global botnets of infected computers with tremendous power to collect information or take down an entire company. Centrally controlling hundreds of thousands or even millions of systems, the hacker (also referred to as a "herder") will direct these systems to send out spam for advertising, spam for malicious code distribution, or may set up a business that distributes illegal pedophilia material from your system; something you might actually be indicted for.

Botnets are also used to carry out large scale denial of service attacks (sending millions of requests to one company's web application simultaneously in an attempt to overload and shut down that system) for purposes of extortion or to take out the competition. The point is, these criminals are not using their own systems to carry out these illegal activities but rather your internal systems. At some point someone has to ask the question, who is liable for the crimes committed through these corporate owned systems? Technology is going to be pointing to you, not the hacker controlling your system.

Experts tell us that hackers are expanding their targets for different types of information as new schemes are developed. Key targets include health related data, internal corporate notes and Outlook accounts, and FTP (file transfer protocol) services that can be used to access intellectual property as well as government facilities. This is no longer just an attack on banks and credit card databases.

Understanding Information Theft

Earlier I mentioned a group called Shadowcrew. If you visit shadowcrew.com, chances are you'll receive a message that states: "This domain is parked, pending renewal or has expired. Please contact the domain provider with questions." Not much there, right? But on May 30, 2005, *Businessweek Online* described this group as an organized crime syndicate that used identity information to perpetrate fraud. Secret service agents worked out of a high-tech command center and observed the cybercrime gang on twelve digital screens resembling a war-room. Operation Firewall was created to track down and arrest this group of people trained in identity theft, money laundering and the resale of stolen information.

Shadowcrew was one of the first information theft gangs to emerge, using illegal sites similar to eBay

"At 9 p.m., Nagel, the Secret Service's assistant director for investigations, issued the "go" order. Agents armed with Sig-Sauer 229 pistols and MP5 semi-automatic machine guns swooped in, aided by local cops and international police." The result: "Twenty-eight members were arrested, most still at their computers."

According to BusinessWeek's article, these groups are winning: "They are stealing more money, swiping more identities, wrecking more corporate computers, and breaking into more secure networks than ever before." The damages from these groups continue to grow into the millions.

Online information brokers like ShadowCrew.com take information and turn it into cash before account owners can react. It would have been easy for Brian Salcedo to take the Lowe's credit card numbers, visit "hacker" chat rooms and find brokers who, for the right price, would turn them into fraudulent cards. It's an astoundingly quick process that should not be underestimated.

Stolen data can be used in a variety of ways. Buyers purchase credit card or account numbers, then research to fill in missing elements such as maiden names to open an account. Then perpetrators can obtain additional credit cards, take out cash advances or qualify for loans, and even make large purchases in your name. Then they disappear and leave your name behind with large unpaid debts.

In recent years, medical organizations have become a target as organized crime syndicates have discovered ways to cash in. In one case, thieves accessed medical files of Maria Shriver, Britney Spears and George Clooney in a scam that turned out to be very lucrative. According to USA Today, these thieves where able to use medical information to acquire new credit cards, drain bank accounts and submit claims to insurance companies. While this information is often encrypted (and HIPAA laws require certain security controls to be in place), insiders can gain access to this information without actually hacking into anything. Going after medical records is easier than gaining access to bank accounts, and by fraudulently billing the insurance companies, a thief can generate hundreds of thousands of dollars with little questioning.

In April 2007 a former New York Presbyterian Hospital employee had assisted thieves in gaining access to over 50,000 patient records, according to an article published on May, 2007 in *USA Today*. Once this happens, patients may find they are responsible for bills they never incurred, while the thief is long gone.

Small Businesses are at Risk Too

While it makes sense that hackers want to gain access to large companies, it's not always easy to draw the same conclusions when dealing with the small to medium business (SMB) community. The risks, however, are real. The same people who carry out large-scale jobs are also attacking SMB companies, generally using more automated approaches that reach out to just about any company or individual.

How Information is Stolen

Cybertheives use our computers as satellites to do their dirty work. They hijack them and set them up for future illegal exploits. We remain in possession of the computer, likely unaware of the second user, but the system can be redeployed in an instant to act as a relay for an attack against government resources or break into banks. The hackers can commit a wide array of crimes that can be traced back to the owner's system. The attacker could be anywhere in the world, but law enforcement officials will initially think the attack originated from your system. Imagine how embarrassing it would be if the FBI showed up at your doorstep early one morning with a warrant to search for child pornography distribution applications.

It's foolish to think Microsoft's new operating system, or perhaps Symantec's new anti-spyware software, will make them pack up his business and go into something else. Again, these technologies play an important role in security, but are no match as independent safeguards.

The simple act of opening up electronic cards, downloading free music and videos or clicking the link sent by the con can introduce bots into your system that will later to be used to access key corporate assets. Once the Trojan in installed, the game is over. The hacker is in and can disguise his tools and tricks to avoid discovery; even to the point of hiding from automated security analysis tools.

Now you have an understanding of how information is stolen and what is happening in the world of information security—and how it impacts the areas you manage. This knowledge will allow you to direct the security strategies needed by your company.

For the IT manager, you will discover how to explain to managers and data owners how information theft is destroying company reputations and customer trust, diminishing shareholder value, eating away at market share, and even causing business failures, personal fines and jail time. If you can prove to data owners that their systems are being compromised, you will seriously help your company before it's too late.

If a company has data that merits buying computers and networks, this company's data is worth protecting. The question is: Does your company understand the risks involved in failing to take the appropriate actions to secure his systems and data? Let's get started with building an asset mindset toward securing that data.

Dave Stelzl

Chapter 3

Why Security Fails

People spend very little money and time protecting their most valuable financial asset, their identity.

John Sileo, *Stolen Lives*

Strong security is a system, not a product. Various aspects of security work together to create a series of responses, so that when security does fail, and it will, there is a back up to catch unauthorized attempts before data is compromised, misused or stolen.

Good security is also a discipline comprised of policies, standards, guidelines and procedures; think of it as a protocol. The success of security depends in many ways on the people using and administering digital assets, and on well designed interaction between these people and technology safeguards.

Security is dynamic; it must be able to respond to changing circumstances and able to predict things that might happen, or respond to the unexpected. This requires smart people who understand what assets are and the policies that govern them.

People are helpful. As Kevin Mitnick writes in his book, *The Art of Deception*, companies are looking for team players and helpful people. Administrative people don't want to be known as obstacles, always getting in the way of progress. Companies use security badges, but they might not be checked every morning when employees come in to work. And only the security guards check these out. But imagine an elderly woman carrying several boxes of food in preparation for a departmental meeting. How do you know if that lady works there? Even if you recognize her from previous mornings, she may have gotten the pink slip yesterday and no longer is counted among the badged employees. In fact, she might be coming back to create a disruption, disguising herself as an employee, but armed with hammers and spray paint after a wrongful termination.

Technology is rigid. It is not polite; it insists on checking every badge, and when someone is standing out in the cold having forgotten their badge, there is no mercy. Sometimes this rigid approach back-fires. Between human kindness and other character issues, and the rigid, calculated side of technology, there is a gap in the system that will cause security to fail. Every system has a weakness, and it is at this point that your security will fail. We need to understand, based on the last chapter, where your focus needs to be as you develop a new mindset across the company's asset owners, users and administrators.

Around the turn of the century (which sounds like a long time ago, but is just short of a decade now), the big hype in security was zero day response. Companies scrambled to find ways of detecting an attack the moment it hit. They hoped that others would get hit first, so updates would be released in time to stop the attack at their company, similar to running just a little faster than the person behind you in a bear chase.

How does security fail? Often it's some sort of operator error – someone internally printing secure information in the wrong place, setting up an insecure server, or creating an open door through peer to peer networking. Of course with the paperless office, there are always reports of discarded hard copies put in the trash unshredded.

So there is a technology side to this security dilemma, but there is also a data user side.

The Point of Attack

Data users are often what we'd consider knowledge workers. They have a function within the company either creating, fulfilling, or supporting revenue generating activities. Their jobs often involve the creation and usage of important digital assets. They also represent the weakest point in your security architecture.

Attackers rarely come head-on. Instead, they look for the weak areas knowing that all security must have a door in the system if the data is going to be used by someone. A house that is completely secure cannot be lived in. I was in the airport recently and watched a team of police officers stand guard over an ATM machine as it was restocked. The money stacks sat in plastic bags on the floor while a separate team of men opened the machine. One thing was obvious to everyone, this machine was well guarded. This is an example of an **interface** in security processes. The machine itself is fairly secure, but it must be unlocked and opened for periodic maintenance and restocking. This process is where security interfaces come together creating a weak point and it is here that attacks will happen; if someone is trying to get in.

While working on this chapter, I was flying to Philadelphia. The man sitting next to me brought up the topic of airport security. He used to be on the terrorist list which meant that he had to show up early at the airport to get his ticket in person. He explained, people on the terrorist list have to be checked in by a human, not a kiosk. But when US Airways merged with America West, the list was apparently lost. He now flies just like I do. The merging of the two airlines created a huge hole in security.

Professional attacks focus on interfaces that join various aspects of security, creating such a weak point. I recently read about an international from China who went to school in the states, received an engineering degree, and took a job with an organization doing government classified work. He was arrested for espionage. This seems time consuming, but some criminals have exhibited an inordinate amount of patience if the reward is big enough. This opens up a pretty big hole in our security program. A temp agency might be another way to gain authorized access. Who is to say that the new telephone operator doesn't have a master's degree in programming and connections with the underground?

The point is there are an unlimited number of holes in any security plan; too many to predict which one will be used next.

Security is a System

I am certain someone has a book out there with a complex and technically accurate definition of security, but for ease of discussion let's define security as a system or a framework used to describe a set of procedures with technology and people. They work in concert to guard against a loss of privacy, confidentiality or availability. You could picture the line of defense in football that uses several players working together. This system might be comprised of a single organism, it might include organizations, or it may refer to a number of components working together. In our corporate world, it will generally be a combination of people and technology working together.

Systems that Occur Naturally Work Best

Early discoveries of systems generally refer back to those existing naturally in the science disciplines. One of the early areas of system studies (to my knowledge) is found in biology. These biology systems relate well to the topic of security, so let's learn from them.

When we take any component out of its system, it doesn't seem to function as it should. For example, you can't remove any component from the immune system if you want it to still function correctly.

The immune system was designed to work in concert with many other systems in the body such as hormones which may, if not in balance, actually attack the immune system. But when working together naturally, the systems of the body each do their job and keep a person healthy.

A naturally occurring system is somewhat seamless, although there can be many complications. There are necessary things a person must do to maintain their body and its systems, but overall they tend to function, while slowly breaking down as we grow in age. This system is flexible and responsive and works against most normal attacks, but like any system, it can be overloaded and made to fail.

Man-Made Systems

Mechanical systems designed and built by humans also carry out functions as components working together. However, in most of these mechanical systems, weaknesses naturally occur where components are brought together. Consider airplanes; everything about the aircraft has been designed to provide high-powered, lightweight and fast transportation from one destination to another. There are thousands of systems here working together to make this thing fly. Even the toilet in the back of the plane is a complex system that has to work just right. There is an entire section in the Airframe and Power Plant manuals explaining how it operates and how to troubleshoot it.

Aircraft naturally encounter tremendous vibrations during takeoff, flight and landing. One small problem could put many lives in jeopardy, and of course will have a tremendous impact on the business of that airline.

Aviation A&P mechanics tell us that vibration is the number one enemy of these systems. Where components come together, there is a constant level of vibration that threatens to break the seams that connect these components. One of the many safeguards is small gauge safety wire threaded through the head of any critical bolt, twisted a specified number of times and then attached to a nearby flange. Now, when vibration occurs, the bolt cannot be undone. Maintenance workers have to actually cut this wire to remove the bolt.

Security systems occur both in biology as well as electro-mechanical systems built by humans. Just like the plane example, these man-made systems have major weaknesses at the seams. When components are used to secure data without consideration for the overall system, we end up with security that doesn't really work. When we increase the number of components that don't naturally integrate together, we tend to decrease security.

Professional attackers study these systems in an effort to find the weak links. While hacking through firewalls may present a challenge and some level of fun for bored technologists, the professional will likely bypass this time wasting activity and break through barriers at one of the seams. Why hack in when you can just call someone and ask for the password?

These seams exist all over the company. Some are related to people, others technology. Badge security is fairly effective in protecting an office building. "Piggy backing" on someone with a badge is almost always a good strategy if one can keep from looking obvious. This ruse is especially effective in larger organizations where people don't know everyone.

These seams also occur when a safe is opened at a bank, money is moved by truck (loading and unloading), or where applications and technology interface with each other. People using laptops that encrypt data going to the office can feel pretty good about the encryption. It would be hard for hackers to crack the code, although it's not impossible. But why bother when you can simply see it on the screen while standing behind the person (a practice called shoulder surfing)? Or hackers can send users an email containing Trojan code that would allow them to see your computer from a distance.

Security fails when people have focused on components rather than systems. The technology mindset is to spend inordinate time on the firewall or VPN technology, with little consideration for laptop security or end user awareness training.

In security briefings you may hear me say, "You could get rid of your firewall and have the same level of security you have now." There's some hyperbole here, but the essence of what I am saying is, the firewall provides a false sense of security. It keeps out floods of rogue traffic, but not professional hackers.

Security is a Discipline

Security is a system, but it is also a discipline much like establishing a habit of daily exercise. These disciplines often interact with a system, like the discipline of healthy living has major positive effects on the immune system as well as every other system in your body. The opposite is true, as we all hear and read. Many suffer from adrenal fatigue, which comes with not dealing properly with stress, which leads to all kinds of health problems. Some doctors may treat the symptoms, focusing on surface issues, but not identifying the root cause which may be stress or nutrient imbalances that created underlying adrenal fatigue.

A workaholic and hyper-organized office worker may write down a daily list of to-dos, but over time realize that their life is out of balance. They have given an inordinate amount of time and energy to work, looking back only to find that their marriage and family has fallen apart. Balancing life takes discipline. Writing this book was certainly a product of discipline. No one sits down and writes a book; rather it takes a vision, then goals along the way, and the scheduling of time to research, write, edit, and rewrite over the course of many months and sometimes years.

Security is also a discipline that works on a system comprised of technology and people components working together to achieve a predictable outcome. We will look more at the system of security when we explore how security actually works in the next chapter.

Like time management disciplines, security is a daily discipline. Every discipline starts with education. No one is going to take the time to exercise if they don't understand the benefits. Stephen Covey discusses, in *Seven Habits,* the need for regular exercise as part of that life balance – in other words he actually includes disciplines of health and relationships as part of his overall time management system. His eye opening comments suggest that people don't feel like they have time for exercise, and I am no exception, and yet he adds that you can't afford the time *not* to exercise. I believe this, so I have developed a discipline of daily exercise.

Security requires educating data owners and data users on the relevant threats to corporate secrets and application availability. This is not a onetime thing, either, but an ongoing process of keeping people up to date and aware of what is happening, and what could happen as new developments are discovered, business climate changes, and global threats come and go. Assessing risk is another discipline that must be carried out more often than it generally is. Then there are cultural disciplines like making sure people have badges and reporting or questioning those who do not, signing in, asking questions, maintaining control of your personal workspace, hard copy data and files, and access to your computer, such as screen saver passwords when you leave your desk, or maintaining control of your laptop while traveling. Security fails when these disciplines are overlooked or people become complacent.

Natural Weak Points

All security systems have weak points. I would argue that in many ways, man made security systems have more weak points and are generally easy to compromise.

Why? Because these systems are comprised of human and technology controls which are integrated together, and each interface or seam in the system is a possible weakness. Assets too cannot be seen as a single entity because they are also in a sense, systems. These systems also have seams which create weaknesses in the overall system and security.

As we continue the migration to more electronics and more complex systems, the systems naturally become less secure – in this case the asset systems become too complex to easily secure, and the security system becomes somewhat unmanageable or laden with bugs. For instance, in the past we physically signed for many things that now require only a card scan. Clerks used to check credit card signatures more routinely, but now only check occasionally, even though the machine clearly says, "hand card to clerk." Online ordering is another example of technology growing more complicated. It never required a signature, resulting in a new breed of security problems, so there is now the added requirement for your three digit security code – something that has actually improved the authentication process.

The biggest naturally occurring weakness, in my opinion, comes when the assessor does not understand the boundaries of the system, or hidden aspects of it. The entire system must always be considered because professional hackers will likely know where some of the hidden nuances lie. Start by asking where the data is, what systems interface with the obvious system, who accesses this data, from where, and with what? Then you'll see that a given system is much larger than initially thought. In the age of business intelligence applications and ad hoc reporting, we see data routinely taken from a primary system in the form of a subset and placed in less secure environments such as portable data repositories, mobile computing devices, or simply emailed home for some late night work. These portable computing devices must all be considered as part of the system, and likely represent the greatest seams and weaknesses in the system.

As mentioned earlier, criminals will find out where executives live and park outside their homes to tap into their wireless networks (war driving). This little trick bypasses IT security and goes right to weak point in the system – the home of a non-technical asset owner. Once on the wireless network, it's not hard to access the prized data, and perhaps even gain access to the corporation by infiltrating that home computer and waiting for them to access the corporate network from home.

This is exactly what I mean when I say asset owners do not realize how large their system is. Part of securing this system should be educating the execs of the risks involved in working over unsecured wireless networks. This includes the wireless routers we use to access the Internet throughout the house. Security fails when people aren't educated.

The Fallacy of "Good Security"

You can't actually test security. You can run some attacks, try out the functions, and look for things that don't work or bugs that can be exploited in the software. But when you look at many of the attacks over history, they tend to target the unexpected or obscure aspects of the system, things people just didn't think about in the production cycle or the building of the system. In fact, the professional hackers spend most of their time thinking about the attack and very little of the time actually performing it. Their efforts are spent figuring out what you missed, and then working out an effective strategy that will leverage these discovered weaknesses. The attacker clearly has the advantage here.

Years ago I was responsible for a software development testing team. We put together many scenarios and tested various modules for months. In doing this job, I soon discovered that there are such an enormous number of permutations for things that can happen that there isn't a way to run every scenario - not even close. We would first use the system for things it was designed for, entering data sets provided by programmers, users, and testers to make sure the system does what it's supposed to do. Then we entered data that didn't make sense, or we didn't fill in all the fields or overloaded them. We'd turn things off in the middle or try to crash the system. Of course I am giving you a quick overview and leaving out many of the boring details of testing. At the end of the day, however, you can't really try all types of hardware, add-on software, and interactions with other applications that may be tried by a thief.

In fact, if changes are made during the testing process, or when steps are taken to fix or improve the system or security, we often end up with a lesser product – one fix caused a different problem. Take airport security for instance. LoJack (a service users can subscribe to assist with stolen laptop recovery) tells us that a laptop is stolen every 50 seconds. I like to maintain control of my laptop while at the airport at all times, however now I am forced to put it on a belt where I can't see it for at least a minute, long enough for someone to grab it. A minute may not seem long, but with hundreds of black cases going through the machine, it's hard to keep track of it. I do my best to watch when it goes in, and then I race through the metal detector before it comes out, but not everyone is as paranoid as I am.

Laptop scanning is an example of making a change in security that created a new problem. This one change in turn may create much bigger problems on the other end. This is especially problematic when the original issue was something very unlikely, while the new issue is something commonplace. A bomb inside a laptop is probably rare, but laptops are commonly stolen. (So maybe a different way to check them would make more sense.)

Security systems present some serious challenges when it comes to testing. Consider a large scale disaster like a nuclear power plant melt down. Sure, we can build some sort of simulation to predict what would happen, but as we've seen in history, it doesn't always work the way we imagine it will. The same has been true for some of the space shuttle accidents. In between these larger disasters, we have the everyday systems that support the assets of your company. Even on this smaller scale, it's hard to know if your computer systems will be up and running tomorrow morning or if your tapes really will restore if something fails.

I worked with an internationally recognizable manufacturer several years ago on a recovery project, and they'd been backing up the system in question to tape on a daily basis. Our team conducted an assessment and recommended replacing the current tape system due to some questions concerning reliability. The cost was too high for them, so the recovery process relied on this questionable system. Not long after the assessment, this particular system, which was critical to their manufacturing process in the generators division, crashed. It didn't restore. We had to fly the crashed disk to California which ended up costing about $30,000. The disk of course had to be replaced, but the big cost was shutting down a 7 by 24 production facility for three days. In the end, the tape upgrade would have been well worth the cost.

In the case of cybercrime, the likelihood of considering every possibility is far less. While we can predict and mitigate many of the operational and technical failures, it is impossible to know what an attacker is thinking. Professional criminals, if they are experienced, look and test the systems to see what countermeasures have been put in place and then attack at the weak points. The attacker simply has to discover what guards are up and attack the holes. Again, the attacker has the advantage here. In many cases a class attack can be developed that works across many different companies due to some common software bug or website issue, and can be automated to penetrate many companies without the attacker actually targeting a specific company. The mindset that "we are not a target" is a wrong mindset when dealing with class attacks and automation.

Instead a company should assess the largest holes, consider the most valuable assets and watch closely for noises that might be made as an attack begins. Technology always seems to favor the attacker while the good guys are trying hard to catch up.

Attackers also have an advantage in that most defenders lack real world security experience. The adage "practice makes perfect" is a good one here. People who are constantly responding to situations learn to respond the right way, but not many people have had that experience. What about the people who haven't encountered an attack? Or maybe they've seen several, but not the one hitting your company. Security fails because people don't know how to respond in time. That's why I'll soon discuss building a mindset that is alert and ready to respond.

Technology vs. People

Another issue is understanding the balance of people and technology: Which is better? Which does our company rely on most?

Technology

Technology relies on computers which are very good at some things, and not so good at others. The real value of computer systems is the ability to do something over and over without ever becoming bored or without making a mistake, if programmed to do it right the first time. So if something is working, you can count on the computer doing it that way forever, unless someone disrupts it or some software or hardware failure occurs. Of course there are always bugs in the software and sequences that cause computers to fail eventually. Hardware will always fail at some point. It's just a matter of time.

Security technology focuses on defending against predictable attack methods, often with little regard for the actual assets. With preprogrammed responses in place, computers attempt to defend against an unlimited number of attack methods, many of which are unknown at any point in time. Counter to this, attackers will use all types of attack methods to achieve the desired goal – a goal the defender may have no knowledge of. The defender is left to predict the next attack idea, and the result is a game of catch up; an unwinnable game in many cases.

So when creating a security routine, the programmer predicts what might happen and then creates an automated defense against it. An example is a virus signature that can be detected through software that watches packets of data coming through from the Internet, waiting for something that looks like an attack. This process is known as pattern matching. Consider a computerized chess game that uses the game tree concept. It checks your last move against every possible move it can make, then checks what moves you will be able to make for each option. The computer will check more levels as the game grows more sophisticated. This is why harder levels of computer chess take longer to play – the computer takes time to go through all of these options while you wait.

The problem comes when the human player becomes so proficient that you remember what the computer will do in certain situations. In other words, it is possible for you, the human player, to learn ways of tricking the computer at lower levels of playing simply by remember what sequences of moves cause the computer to make a certain move. Once you figure this out, you might as well move on to a new level because the computer will make the same mistake every time – after all, it's a computer that has no capability to reason or understand. Note that it also doesn't care who wins the game.

The same is true for security technologies. Once the hacker figures out a sequence of entries on a webpage, or writes a new virus that has yet to have a signature or known pattern, they will win every time until the software provider figures out the mistake and provides an update. Computers cannot react to new situations. So the more automated we get, the less security we have in many ways. Consider a wire transfer. It used to be that bankers knew their clients and you had to speak to someone you knew to transfer money (this may be going way back in history). Just yesterday one of my workshop attendees told me how someone stole his banking account and routing numbers and was able to successfully order a money transfer of $105,000 to another account that he did not know about or have access to. The criminal, to date, has not been found. When questioned, the bank admitted to my client that this was a hole in the system.

Similar to the computer in a chess game, an attacker begins to learn the programmed security responses and gains a predictable advantage. He can count on the computer responding the same way every time, which he learns by making the system respond over and over until he understands the automated response program. Then he simply finds a way around this. Since security is something that must be running all the time, the attacker gets to pick a point in time, test the system, and then back away to see what happens. The defender, in this case the IT staff, may look to see what is happening, but by the time he gets the alert and checks on it, there may be nothing to see. Someone probed the system, but is gone. Over time our assailant grows in his understanding of the security system and avoids the responses he has learned.

This also works for an intrusion detection alert. The attacker comes in at night, setting off an alarm every Sunday night at 2 AM for a month or two. After a while the security person who is getting paged in the middle of the night decides there is some type of bug in the system (Or maybe their spouse who gets awakened each Sunday night makes the decision for them). Now the alarm is disabled and the attacker is free to go in.

People

People are generally better than technology at providing security; however, they have two major flaws; they become bored and they tend to give in to courteous people that seem to have good intentions. Going back to my example of nuclear power. In order to maintain a safe operating environment, the plant hires highly trained people to observe the ongoing operations of the plant. The problem is nothing ever goes wrong. One clip I saw on the news showed a couple of men watching some pipes and gauges through a 3 foot thick glass shield. Pretty boring.

Of course I am using some hyperbole again; there are occasional problems, but not enough to keep any highly trained person interested. So they lose focus, quit, or just check out of reality and day dream – perhaps reading a novel. In this situation, security response has taken a back seat. Good security requires a watchful eye. But the likelihood of an incident is high only over long periods of time – and the timing is nearly impossible to predict. Sitting there, waiting for a failure to happen, can be a daunting task. Who will watch with anticipation every second?

A second problem, which we have already alluded to, is the general helpfulness of people who want to be seen as team players. We have been taught not to question authority in larger corporations or to question people walking the halls. Also note that people gossip about the security guy who is always cranky and insists that everyone show their badge even though he sees them every day. Many large scale attacks include insiders for this reason.

Another problem with people is in the area of ethics. While people are better judges when it comes to response, they may also be untrustworthy. Machines don't lie and can't be bought, people can. Disgruntled employees can be persuaded by thieves to cooperate for a price; it's just a question of how risky the opportunity is. The more automated things become and the less risky they sound, the more likely insiders will agree to be involved.

It would be hard to convince someone to shoot another individual or break in to a house. Even taking something from someone's cubical seems too risky for the average insider. However, turn to automation and there are no people involved. It's no longer a crime against a person, no breaking and entering, and no one (on the surface) gets hurt. The insider's job is often fairly easy such as changing some logs, opening a port or adding some code to a server. Technology has made the crime of stealing seem less personal.

Someone once told me that character is what people do when no one is looking. This is why accounting practices require regular audits, which may find executives cooking the books to make money – they do this while no one is looking. However, in the IT area, there doesn't seem to be as many audits. Individuals have more power than one person should have, making it more tempting to do things that may be considered criminal.

Insiders who are familiar with the inner workings of the company are always hard to stop and may go undetected for years, maybe forever. On the other hand, companies often fail to consider the insider as a real threat. It's hard to believe that someone you know might be involved. It is a common mistake for companies to spend all their efforts guarding the perimeter while the insider attacks. Remember the recent Anthrax scare? This was a knowledgeable insider who had access to the drug that killed those exposed after the 9/11 attack. It seemed like the investigation focused on the Middle East, when in reality it was happening right here in the US government.

Finally, people make judgments that machines just don't make. This can be good as we have discussed. Sometimes we need a judgment call when something happens that a machine can't understand. Sometimes things just don't look right, or someone has a feeling that they act on, and it's right. The flip side of this is that people get used to something and stop watching as we've already discussed, because they are bored or complacent. A great example is in the code levels of the US Homeland Security. I can't remember a time in the airport over the past 2 to 3 years when the code level was not "Code Level Orange." Exactly what does that mean? Do I do something different than I would if it were yellow? I really don't know. In any case, like everyone else, I ignore it.

Automation and Complexity Impede Security

Computers bring automation, which in many cases is good for production. If you had to handwrite every letter that went out to your customer base, you'd give up the idea of growing your business. Running numbers on a spreadsheet makes projections and planning easier, and using a credit card online has made my Christmas shopping much easier. People are calling for more automation, but not all automation is smart, and without proper security, it can be deadly.

Complexity, which is growing as computers become easier to use, is also an enemy of security. When I started in computer science, operating systems were small, applications fairly simple, and networking mostly manual. We had to know how to configure everything, load drivers, set dip switches, and keep track of network addresses on spreadsheets. The entire operating system fit on my 20 MB hard drive, leaving plenty of room for data. You'll need a great deal more just for the operating system today.

The job of configuring and loading has been replaced with "plug and play" technology. My computer operating system has been redesigned to connect to everything. So If I walk into a hotel, it detects any wireless network and asks me if I want to connect. Most people are going to say yes, without considering the consequences. If I plug in a printer or install software, my computer takes over and completes the install. Programs that I have installed get automatically updated, often at night so that it doesn't interrupt my day. While this has made life simple for me, the complexity behind all of this is enormous, and in most cases we have traded functionality for security.

The flip side to helpful automation of course is automated attack methods. Automation has made it possible for people to steal things that in a manual world would be completely safe. You've no doubt heard the idea of stealing a fraction of a cent from many bank accounts, eventually adding up to a large sum. Since account balances are carried out to the thousandths place, one can theoretically round every account balance down to the nearest cent without anyone really taking notice. Doing this once would be meaningless, doing this hundreds of millions of times would add up. Automation has given attackers the ability to conceive a plan that would generally go unnoticed, and do it millions of times over time. The smaller the attack, the less noticeable it is. Hackers avoid the risk of breaking and entering to steal large sums of money in one act, but repeat minuscule thefts millions of time over in a remote location and greatly reduce their risk.

A close cousin to automation is the massive increases in data aggregation; creating larger and more enticing targets for thieves. One can count on any laptop containing valuable data, whether it's

Quicken files that contain account numbers or perhaps bank accessing programs that have been automated. Data users constantly duplicate data sets to work remotely – people don't really work with paper and pencil anymore. It's all automated and kept in one location.

Automation also means anonymity in many cases. When was the last time you really spoke to, or even looked the cash register attendant in the eyes? Most of us approach the counter looking for the computer that reads our card. If you were to engage the attendant, they would likely point you back to the box. Even the signature is electronic in most cases.

"Please Pay the Automated Attendant,
For human assistance, call 1-800-hold4ever"

People are not likely to steal one card online – they want the entire database. They want aggregated info to build an entire profile with. The attacker is ahead, thinking of new scams, meanwhile the defender is always trying to catch up. As systems get more complex and easier to use, we give up security for ease. Compare Windows against the old DOS computers: Windows recognizes and installs almost anything automatically. DOS required all kinds of configuring to get on the network or to add any external device. Complexity is the enemy of security. Automation is a next of kin.

When Security Fails, It Fails Badly

In the September 9, 2008 issue of *USA Today,* Sandra Block explains how credit card fraud is done. It would seem difficult to steal one credit card number and have it be worth much because the owner would certainly spot strange transactions, place an alert on the card, and perhaps track down the assailant.

Block showed how new account fraud has become one of the most pernicious forms of identity theft. The card number is stolen, but rather than actually using it, the thieves use it as support for opening a new account. There is no way to know this is happening without seeing some type of credit report or alert. (Credit alerting programs and lock down has become very popular for this reason). The new card may be set up to go to a new address or PO Box, keeping the criminals anonymous. Detection at this point requires some alerting program.

The goal is to take info, open bank accounts and obtain credit cards in a person's name, get large cash advances, and then disappear, leaving the victim with debt. *USA Today* reported we had about 500,000 cases in 2001 and 8.5 million in 2005, and it has grown from there. It's safe, profitable, and easy – at least it would appear so.

How does your security fail?

Software and hardware must work properly, but given the general user population, they must also be easy to use. So software engineers have focused on building easy to install and easy to use programs that don't require much in the way of training or documentation.

Security, on the other hand, focuses on figuring out how things will fail or be compromised, and then preventing those failures. It requires expertise and creativity to predict what might happen. Still, it's impossible to consider every case and too expensive to try many of the cases we do think up.

In fact, since there are an infinite number of attacks possible, testers understand that everything won't be addressed and they have to send products out knowing there are flaws. The question is, which attacks or problems won't cause much damage, and which ones should hold up production? "Defense in depth" will be part of the solution.

"Defense in depth" is a term security professionals use to ensure that a single vulnerability or weakness cannot compromise the entire security program. So if one device fails, say a firewall, there is something else to catch it. Much of the malicious traffic coming into corporate computers today is permissible in email, downloads of freeware and personal programs, web traffic, and P2P (Peer to Peer) Networking. "Defense in depth" would make sure that traffic that did get past the firewall would be screened by some other device such as intrusion protection technology. There may be additional controls at the desktop to further inspect what is actually getting installed on the endpoint itself.

Also, in well defined security programs, choke points are created to restrict traffic, creating a checkpoint similar to a border guard. Everyone must go through the booth before passing over the border. But with a large border, it is impossible to watch the entire perimeter, especially if there are many direct connections to the outside (for instance having many mobile devices that connect both inside and out). Without choke points there is just no way to watch it all. When these architectural considerations are not used, and often they are not, security will fail.

Failing Safely

The best security does not have single points of failure. In addition to this, security must be built to fail-safe. Fail-safe is a term I first learned in the aviation industry when I was learning to fly. As explored earlier, there are many systems making up an aircraft, and since a problem can result in the loss of engine power or something equally frightening, airplanes are generally designed to "fail safe." In other words, if a system fails, it must fail in a safe way.

A simple example of this for your home computer is its uninterruptible power supply (UPS). It keeps your computer from shutting off abruptly when the power fails. If the UPS has a routine shut down process, it will begin to save any work to a new name so that it can be recovered, shut down all processes in a orderly fashion, and then power down before the UPS battery is drained. If the power comes on quickly enough, none of this will be necessary and the system will remain operational. Security systems fail poorly when they don't fail safe.

False Positives

Another type of security failure is when an alarm sounds without any real problem. If the UPS began the shut down process without a power outage, you'd probably be pretty upset. False positives are in a way more damaging than some security breaks. If the system continually shuts down without a power outage, you will likely disconnect the UPS or disable the software responsible for making this happen. Hackers know this and will sometimes trigger responses on purpose to get you to do this.

Security is a complex thing. Since nothing works all of the time, there has to be a balance between security that seems too sensitive, like a glass break alarm that is triggered by someone dropping a pencil, and not being sensitive enough and allowing a burglar to quietly cut the class and gain entrance. Failures must trigger the alarm at just the right time if they are going to be useful. If the alarm goes off too often, like car alarms, no one will pay attention. Systems fail poorly when they don't fail at the right time.

When security only addresses part of the system – it's bad.

Systems fail badly when the entire system is not considered. Most security seems to be built in silos. The Data owners are not talking to data security and the data users are assuming all is well. The entire system must be considered. When security is implemented in silos, the interfaces are weaker. Security may be improved in one area only to weaken another. Data threats may change as business issues arise and go away. All parties involved must understand what is going on, and audits must be used to ensure that people are doing the right things. The entire system includes the technology, the creation of data, where the data is accessed from, where it's stored, how it travels with data users, and a host of other important factors. Does your company consider all of these factors?

Security that inhibits the business fails.

I used to work with a guy who was always complaining about business inhibitors. In some cases it was people, in others it was the choice or lack of the right technology. Putting in security that inhibits business actually inhibits security by causing people to resist it, get around it, or outright fight it.

Placing restrictions on technology use such as IM (instant messaging), email and Internet access don't seem to work either. As technology advancements are made, people learn about them and find ways to apply them to the business. Sometimes this advances production, sometimes it doesn't, but it seems like there is always a technology person waiting to stamp it out without considering its value.

While I am in favor of testing things out, and doing things right, I find that whenever a company quickly reacts to new technology (for instance, "No IM"), they face a big fight with departments that are making money. Then a game of leapfrog ensues, where the company blocks certain protocols while the developers find ways around the blocks. The best solution is to educate users, develop secure ways to use the technology, and build an asset mindset around securing the data. Inevitably people are going to use it at home while working with corporate systems and data, so better to get everyone working together on an appropriate solution.

In the Final Analysis

In the final analysis, security failures stem from just a couple of major root causes. People are the best source of security when they are well trained, well equipped, and focused. Most are not, at least over the long run, and so they do not handle data well, or understand what to do when a system breach occurs. Computers do well with keeping up on logs and data without ever tiring, but they can only do what the programmer has programmed them to do – this of course poses significant limitations.

The security we design can't really be tested. The fine balance between too many false alarms and too little sensitivity to real attacks is a fine line. Tuning this just right is hard to do and requires time and thought. Finally, the trade offs between too much restriction, and too open an environment, are hard to negotiate. In the end, each asset owner must determine what data matters, how much access is required, and then with the input of security savvy professionals, make some hard choices between restrictive computing and risk. Educating everyone on what matters will go a long way to filling in the gaps.

So what is fundamentally wrong with the way we are approaching security, and how do asset owners begin to take practical steps? Gaining an asset mindset is the beginning. Then much of the security process will be clear and the decisions that need to be made will be easier with the proper asset mindset. This is the focus of the remaining chapters. In the next chapter I will provide you with the overarching foundational principles that every asset owner must have to ensure their assets are secure.

Chapter 4

The Executive Guide to Digital Assets

Digital assets are unlike anything corporations have dealt with in the past. Where is your data? You still have it even if someone steals it, so do you know if your data has been stolen? What happens when you delete it? Do you understand the nature of digital assets?

Compliance, security policies, new and pending legislation, liability…the list goes on. All of these concepts are tied to this new type of asset called data.

Of course data has been around for a long time, it's not new. But *threats against* data are, and the treatment of data as an asset that needs to be secured, in the same way that precious stones or trade secrets must be guarded, is a new concept with the advent of Internet computing. Even though data has always been sensitive, it is only the last five or six years that we have seen an all out attack on databases. The level of risk is rising, changing the game and making this asset a wanted asset. New considerations are required; a new mindset is needed.

And with this attack has come a continuous stream of regulations, both industry and federal, aiming to protect these assets when companies fail to do it themselves. In recent years medical, financial, accounting and credit card rules have dominated the press.

In every technical workshop I conduct, I always ask, "Who has read or really understands what the security regulations call for?" (Referring to regulations such as PCI, FISMA, GLBA, HIPAA, etc.)

In a class of 20 participants, I can count on there being one— perhaps two. Having taken this poll two or three times a week over the last year, I'm confident technologists are struggling to contribute in this area – and for many, an audit is a fearful thing. If I ask asset owners and executives if they are compliant with the regulations, I get a similar response. I believe the lack of response represents some of the complexity in this area. Where are all of these compliance regulations coming from? Why is it so hard to understand what is called for, and why don't the makers of these regulations realize how expensive and time consuming these requirements are?

So, how important is compliance? And how should companies approach the security of their digital assets while also meeting the requirements set forth by government and industry regulations?

Compliance is a major issue. Companies across the United States are working hard to comply with regulations, including Sarbanes-Oxley (SOX), Gramm-Leach-Bliley (GLBA) and The Health Insurance Portability and Accountability Act (HIPAA). Note: Make sure you know the difference between a HIPPO and HIPAA, and that you don't try to implement HIPPA. As companies take on these challenges, it's important for technology staff and providers to understand who's driving these initiatives, how they will impact technology changes within an organization, and how policies and procedures will be affected.

In this chapter, we'll examine some of the regulations, but we'll take a closer look at the real issues facing IT organizations and data owners. Issues that deal with the data asset, what it is, where it is, and why it is so hard to secure it.

And while this is not a thorough manual on building policies and achieving compliance, we will explore, at a high level, the significance of security policy and governance, asset security, and how to think about an asset unlike the physical assets you are used to working with.

Compliance and Governance

My goal is not to make your company compliant, but rather to give you some structure to think about asset compliance and security. Then you can think ahead on what really needs to be in place as laws change and regulations come into effect.

The real value of compliance is that it has provided a heightened awareness among corporate leaders, asset owners, and data users. However, the growing number of new federal and industry regulations all seems to be focused on information theft and misuse, underscoring the growing threat against a company's digital assets. The bottom line: Asset owners must get involved with asset security, risk levels and understanding how likely they are to experience data loss or incur liability. It is no longer an option.

Addressing Compliance versus Threats

Making sure your company complies with current laws may not secure your data from threats. There are several reasons a company builds security or implements security products: response to a breach or incident, an impending threat, an upcoming or failed audit, or an initiative to become compliant in a particular area. In each case, the security initiative or implementation process will differ.

In the case of an incident or impending threat, projects may be rapidly created within the IT group based on some security analysis that brought a major vulnerability to light. The number of security initiatives stemming from actual attacks is diminishing as managers consider their data safe based on what they are observing in-house. Remember that today's hackers do not want to be famous. They simply want to steal your data without you noticing.

Becoming compliant, on the other hand, is often a long, drawn out process involving committees, meetings, managers and perhaps audits. But in the polls I've conducted, neither compliance nor realized threats are really driving companies toward true asset security.

Compliance is often approached by committee and involves business processes, personnel, training and a host of considerations the technology people cannot provide. The committee is frequently led by someone outside of IT—perhaps a compliance officer or department head. Whoever leads the committee, it's not a formal hierarchy as we know it. As such, whatever decisions that are made are not the purview of a single individual. This, of course, creates a long decision making process and may have limited funding available to it. Addressing compliance head on—unless you work in a highly regulated industry —can be a difficult path to securing assets.

It's no wonder companies are struggling to reach a state of security. If the company doesn't see hackers infiltrating their networks or have auditors breathing down their necks, they aren't moving quickly to secure data. This may end in the unfortunate discovery that you are focusing on the wrong areas, and your digital assets really aren't as secure as you thought.

Where Regulations Apply

Almost every company has to comply with some type of regulation. Some are industry regulations, such as Payment Card Industry Regulations (PCI), which apply to all companies storing credit card information. Twelve items are specified on the VISA and MasterCard websites, similar to the twelve items required under VISA's original Card Information Security Program (CISP).

HIPAA, while closely associated with medical organizations, may also apply to large corporations that store patient health care information in company systems as part of an infirmary, fitness program or employee assistance program. State and local government accounts will maintain HIPAA-regulated data (or patient health care information, known in the industry as PHI) through the school infirmary and prisoner health records. These are just a few examples to consider when thinking through your security plans.

Reading the Regulations

Unfortunately, reading all of the regulations proves to be a frustrating experience. Whether it's SOX, GLBA, HIPAA or another federal regulation, finding a specific infrastructure technology to use can be a daunting task. Manufacturers and technology consultants have been using lines like, "We can solve 'X' problem with 'Y' product" for years, but none of these products are actually mentioned in the regulations, which are vague and complicated. They don't call for any particular infrastructure security solution, making compliance initiatives based on federal compliance a difficult and confusing task.

That said, a new approach is needed—one that does not require the managers to memorize the thousands of regulations. It should also take the liability for compliance off of the asset owner's shoulders. Now, since I am not a lawyer, make sure you compliance officers are involved and that your company is set up to meet auditors when questions are asked. So my goal here is not to create the plan but rather to inject some ideas into the process that may ease the pain of securing these assets, and at the same time provide an easy way to answer auditors.

Instead of learning about each regulation and putting in hours of research, let the committee perform this task. Let your lawyers be concerned with the legal side of it.

But as an asset owner, it is your job to understand the data assets important to the company, their value to the company, and where and how they are used within and outside the company. Your job is to direct technology focused teams to apply the appropriate security controls (policies, procedures, and technology) that will reduce the likelihood of a security breach. Remember, this is not a technology issue, but rather a people issue. In fact, the best security solutions come from a distributed approach that allows data owners to influence how these assets get secured, then working with centralized groups such as IT security to implement various aspects of the program.

One more important point here: Security requirements dictated by a committee to meet compliance laws are not equivalent to making a system secure. Additional security controls will likely be needed if the system is to be considered secure from today's cyber-threats.

Three Principles

Three key principles can be used to simplify the process and create effective security and also leverage the awareness and concern that compliance has brought at the executive level. At the same time we can use these concepts to gain a better understanding of the asset itself: the data. Through the remainder of this chapter, I will explore these three principles from an asset as well as a compliance viewpoint.

Principle #1: Understanding Due Care

Due care means taking reasonable steps to secure data based on the value and sensitivity of that data. Regulations surrounding sensitive information have been around as long as anyone can remember; however, data security regulations have come into light with much greater intensity in recent years due to the exponential rise in computer theft and crime. The more stories we hear about data theft that impacts individuals, the more we can expect the government to introduce new legislation forcing companies to take action. I suppose we would have less of this if companies were preemptive with security, but the fact is, most are not.

Where there are regulations and data, there is liability. That liability can be on the company as well as an individual, and that individual is most likely going to be the asset owner, not the ones charged with custodial responsibility of the asset. This is an important point. As security requirements grow, asset owners often look to IT administrators for the entire answer, when it is not their jurisdiction or liability. While it is likely IT will play a key role in building the technology portion of the information security architecture, they cannot possibly create the overall security strategy. It is not within their jurisdiction or experience to do this.

Take for instance the creation and implementation of the corporate disaster recovery plan (DRP). While DRP does have a great deal to do with the data center, core databases, applications, and networks, the primary focus of DRP is in the safety of your company's people in the event of a real disaster. This is also outside of the IT's jurisdiction and liability.

Defining Due Care

"Due care" deals with taking reasonable steps to secure data. There are more technical (or perhaps esoteric) definitions of due care, but to keep it usable, let's keep it simple.

Due diligence and due care are two terms that are often confused in the disciplines of information security. I frequently hear them used interchangeably, but they are clearly different.

Due diligence can be thought of as an assessment process. Many regulations call for a proper assessment of some kind, so it's important to conduct one. But liability is not associated with assessment. In fact, an assessment's scope is not well defined and therefore cannot be easily targeted for noncompliance.

Due care, on the other hand, *is* associated with liability. This is about taking action on the information found in the assessment. The data owner must understand what it means to demonstrate due care in guarding corporate assets, as well as the reasonable steps that must be taken to secure assets or data. Put simply, due care involves using reasonable controls to protect data or reduce risk.

Per case law, if an incident lands a company in court, the court would review decisions regarding negligence in data treatment. The data owner would be asked to prove he took reasonable action steps to secure his data. An industry expert may be hired to define these reasonable steps.

Due care: Taking reasonable steps to secure corporate data.

If the case involved a manufacturer of bricks, the court might ask the expert witness about minimal requirements, and a simple firewall might be deemed adequate. If the manufacturer was involved in building weaponry for the U.S. military, reasonable steps would be far more stringent. The greater the value or sensitivity of the data, the more stringent the security plan must be.

How Do We Address the Regulations?

I'm not a lawyer, so I urge managers to avoid addressing regulations independently. Rather, it's your job to educate the people involved with the data you own about due care. Data users and data administrators must understand the value and sensitivity of the information they are dealing with. This in turn should drive the level of training, access control, and oversight needed as they perform work related to the data in question.

Because regulations usually do not specify any infrastructure technology, moving toward due care is the safer way to go. In addition, regulations will change over time, as will threats. As your data security needs change, practicing due care and evaluating through due diligence will protect you from legal negligence.

In the coming chapters, I'll provide a simple way to look at security architecture to ensure due care is taken. We will also look at some simple examples of due diligence, providing a management view of due diligence, and a way to involve and evaluate third party organizations offering to perform this risk measurement service.

Principle #2: Applying the ILM Framework

After understanding due care, it's important to see how digital assets work and fit in with technology, policy and procedure, and user awareness to form the bigger picture of making an organization secure and compliant.

Over the last decade, storage companies have made the concept of Information Life-cycle Management (ILM) popular. They've discussed it with executives and data owners, emphasizing the need for different levels of availability, backup and recovery, cost per megabyte and distinct performance levels from various media. I understand why they use this model; however, ILM is a security concept at its core.

ILM refers to the life cycle of data, which starts with creating an asset, continues through the life of that data and ends with either a plan to archive it forever or eventually end its life through data disposal or destruction. Looking at the information life-cycle management stages, you can see a number of things that should be factored into the security strategy you are building. Once again, at this point you should not be thinking about technology solutions, but rather about the asset itself.

Asset owners must consider each stage along with its risks as it changes at each inflection point, as shown in the following illustration.

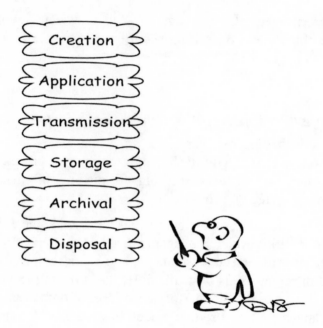

Creation

Data assets are created everyday – perhaps every minute of every day. The intellectual capital your company owns is an asset, and perhaps, as Mack Hanan writes, "the only margin sustaining asset your company has." Company secrets, customer records, formulas, procedures, resources and more all represent some type of asset, and in most cases will exist somewhere in digital form.

As people make phone calls and leave voice mail, send email or correspond with instant messaging, these digital assets are being created. Spreadsheets, database entries, electronic documents, and other electronic media which may be written, audio, or video are all some form of digital asset. You might be surprised that half of all this is somewhere in an email, likely unsecure and traveling through wireless networks or over an unsecure Internet connection.

Do you view your stored digital assets the same way as your customers? They may view their personal information as very valuable. The question will be, "How does your company view it?"

Ultimately it is the asset owner's job to consider how important this asset is to the company.

If it is customer data, and you value your customer, you are going to put a high price on their data. The data must then be categorized and managed according to its value. Notice that both the data user and the data administrator have little authority over how this happens. Why? They likely will not understand the liabilities or sensitivity associated with this data unless you educate them. We will talk more about policy in the next section, but policy will help govern (not secure) this asset.

It is also the asset owner's responsibility to categorize this data, which means in the security world, **classify** the information. There are many levels of classification and all should be classified and used according to policies that govern this type of data. The basic idea is to determine several levels of classifications that can be associated with data from "Public" to "Top Secret," which tell data users and data administrators how to treat this asset.

Application

Most assets are associated with an application such as order entry records, electronic medical record systems, a project plan or design document in manufacturing. The asset owner or federal regulations may restrict access to this information by stating who may view, change or delete it. The concepts of identity management come into play here to provide various users with proper authentication and levels of authorization to a given system.

The application is often viewed as an asset within the corporation, because without it your business may not be able to easily function. However, it is important that the asset owner not lose sight of the asset. These are often created by these applications and then used in daily processing.

For example, a doctor's office creates new assets every time a new patient's paper work is entered into the medical records system.

Access to this data is restricted by HIPAA regulations, but should also be governed by the doctor who is ultimately the asset owner.

It may be legal for an administrative person to access it, but this does not mean that person has a clear understanding of its value or will accept liability of misuse. Unless the application prevents them from doing so, they could easily misuse the data or place it in jeopardy.

Take for instance the numerous AGFA records lost on a laptop a few years ago. The employee placed these on a laptop to continue after hours work. This employee saw leaving this data in the car (in a laptop) as a two or three thousand dollar risk, or the cost of a new laptop, when in fact the data was worth much more. The asset owner knew this, but not the data user. The liability was significant and the loss irrecoverable.

In an even larger case in 2007, the (UK) government had to disclose it had lost the personal records of 25 million individuals, including their dates of birth, addresses, bank accounts and national insurance numbers in the mail, opening up the threat of mass identity fraud and theft from personal bank accounts. In this incident, an administrative person did their normal job and copied the data from an application to a disk and mailed it to a third party. The employee viewed this highly sensitive data, involving over seven million families, as a disk worth a few pounds rather than coveted information worth millions on the black market. The mindset here was clearly wrong.

Transmission

Every system today involves some sort of transmission through LAN, WAN and wireless or other courier services, and this is where many of the security problems start to escalate. Data assets are frequently transmitted all over the world as a part of the normal work process. Think of all the ways we access information to work away from the office, to trade information, collaborate, telecommute, or work from home when a child is sick, or after-hours activities are required to meet a deadline. It is not hard to encrypt data, but encryption does not make remote communications secure. We make many false assumptions when we hit "Send." This includes the idea that email is a secure sending method, or that quickly executed transactions will somehow get past criminals unseen Email, Chat and IM are generally insecure unless special steps are taken, and most will not take these steps.

Wireless could be installed more securely if proper steps are taken Often, it is set up as quickly and simply as possible to gain the productivity it offers. Security is a second thought, and one often taken after a compromise has occurred.

And as mobility requirements increase, keep in mind that data users will continue to demand more and more freedom with transmission. They will want wireless LANs and WANs, air cards that provide cellular network access, and connectivity from all types of public facilities; malls to coffee shops, anywhere, anytime.

Storage

Many of the assets we use in day-to-day business are stored in data centers, but not solely there. Data may be on laptops, PDAs or even as copies on web facing applications used by customers and suppliers. Data is stored in many locations, so the trick is keeping up with data integrity and safeguarding it from unauthorized usage and theft.

Storage is also closely tied to mobility. Frequent travelers often find themselves without Internet access and so are forced to either stop working or copy data to a local laptop drive or memory stick.

A number of problems come with this mobility. First and foremost, the opportunity to lose data grows exponentially. Remember how often laptops are stolen? Now think about company laptops that are clearly marked confidential. Criminals see this and covet the secrets that might be present on their systems. Are your data users traveling around with your company logo on their laptop? It's an advertisement to data thieves.

A second problem comes when you consider the difficultly of actually erasing data. While it's easy to lose a file, it is very hard to erase data completely. That is why it's almost always possible to hire (for a large sum of money) a data recovery company in the event of a disaster. The data is still there, even after a drive failure, a system crash, or an accidental deletion. It's even there when you purposely delete it.

With this in mind, data owners should carefully consider what information should be stored and where. One question all merchants should be asking is, "Should we really save the credit card numbers when customers buy things?" I highly discourage this practice. If you have to do it, require more than a password. I should not be able to call up a company employee, convince them I'm an important senior management in the company, and get them to read me that card number. If it's accessible for the data user, it can be stolen by a schemer.

And finally, moving data to Internet accessible storage areas can be a huge mistake. In Mitnick's book, *The Art of Deception*, he describes how the FBI's instruction manual for accessing the National Crime Information Center database was posted online for agent's convenience. He assumes that this data was posted by people who need it, but saw no value in it outside of their job function. He goes on to describe how this information can be used by a savvy hacker to tap into this database. It requires some social engineering, but if it works, I am hoping that someone who has read his book has also taken steps to remove this data.

Before we leave this topic, there is also the problem of printed documentation. We are living in the paperless office world today, however it seems like the more automated we become, the more we print. Computers were supposed to eliminate paper reporting, but in fact, they have increased hard copy documentation exponentially. Now everyone has access to all kinds of information reporting, statistics and printed email. Data users print it, read it, and toss it, because, after all, it is hard to read on small laptop computers screens.

Everyday data users carelessly toss out sensitive reports in the trash knowing a new report will be out in the morning. These reports contain company financials, customer account numbers, phone numbers, email addresses, and the like. Remember how hackers use social engineering to fill in the gaps? All this garbage is their goldmine.

It's likely that your data users have no idea what is classified and what is not when it comes to these reports. After all, these papers are going in the corporate trash bin. How likely would it be for someone to find this amidst the thousands of other documents thrown away on that same day? The truth is, dumpster divers know that the easy hit is in the trash can, and state laws have ruled that trash is no longer your property once it leaves private property. A dumpster in a parking lot or a can on the street is open season.

Studies have found just about everything, including prescription drugs and needles, thrown into public dumpsters. The bottom line is people are watching your trash and will find the information they are looking for. If you don't have a strict policy on shredding, your information is already out there.

Archival

Much of the data from logs, financial reporting and emails are saved for longer periods of time these days in accordance with federal law and internal policy. The process of securely archiving data in a state that is recoverable becomes a concern as data ages. For instance, today a court may subpoena email data, and the company has 90 days to deliver that data. Would the company be able to retrieve specific emails from five years ago? The likelihood is low, given how email is stored. Recovering data and maintaining its integrity requires a good bit of forethought.

Another issue arises when considering where and how to store this information. Companies frequently choose a third party to store archived data, but whether its onsite or at a third party facility, the likelihood that its trustees understand its value is low. Data value changes over time and the policies associated with different classes of data must dictate how and where it is stored. Only the data owner understands the value and need for this data. And only the data owner can educate trustees on how to protect it.

Disposal

Some data must be maintained for seven years, some for ninety-nine years. But at some point, most data should be destroyed. When systems are outdated, and when PDAs and laptop hard drives are replaced, that data must be destroyed. Disposal is governed by policy, covering the liabilities associated with data that may later be in question. The last stage of the data life cycle process introduces some of the greatest risk and liability. It should be well thought out before it's time to delete these assets.

Much of this data resides on personal laptops or PDAs, so while the data is owned by a data owner, the trustee or data user has control of it. In the case of personal systems such as PDAs, the data administrators or IT department both have been cut off from the normal security management function. At some point the data user will sell, donate or lose the system and the data will be released to unknown people. It should be obvious that data thieves understand this and will be watching for systems to hit eBay.

With these six simple steps, you have a framework that can be used to build a security strategy between asset owners, data users, and data administrators, beginning with the creation of an asset.

1. Creation
2. Application
3. Transmission
4. Storage
5. Archival
6. Disposal

Sample discussion questions might include:

How sensitive is this data? Who is allowed to see it?

Who has the authority to view it, change it, delete it or grant access to other users?

Where are the applications that create or use it—and how secure are they?

Where is this data transmitted? Is it used on wireless networks, sent through email over the Internet? Is it encrypted—or should it be? Are there various levels of security among the departments that create it or use it?

How is it stored? How much data can you stand to lose? If your backups occurred last night and your system fails at the end of the next day, would you be able to recreate that data? (For example, a construction supply company might be able to re-key orders from today; however, wire transfers or stock trade applications cannot afford to lose any data.)

How long does data need to be archived? If it is sent to offsite locations, should it be encrypted before leaving the facility?

At what point is the information deleted? Do your policies state this, and are they enforced?

Relating ILM to Compliance Requirements

Security requirements change at each stage of ILM. Different threats exist and appropriate controls are required. Looking at different ILM stages allows us to see what a regulation says about data each step of the way.

For instance, when data is created, it should be classified. While government organizations have been doing this for years, the practice is inconsistent among private-sector organizations. Many popular compliance areas seem to address these stages, specifying how applications should be treated and accessed, where and how information can be transmitted, specifications for storage and archival, and when data can be disposed of. Regulations will vary on these points, but it is the asset owner that must interpret them, with the help of your compliance officer and legal counsel. Data users and administrators shouldn't take on this responsibility simply because they generally don't understand the value of the data. The asset owner's interpretations of each stage of the ILM will then drive how data is classified, how it is used, and will look to IT or outside consultants to ensure that technology exists to enforce governing policies. By using the concepts of information lifecycle management, the asset owner will have an easy-to-remember framework for driving the right security program internally. I will address this in some detail later in Section 2, dealing with mindsets; being digitally aware.

Let's discuss an example of how an asset owner controls information security. Both GLBA regulations for customer account information and HIPAA regulations for health care information require that only certain individuals can have access to the data on a need-to-know basis. This is an application issue. Both laws prohibit data from being transmitted in an insecure fashion, especially outside the organization, in an unencrypted manner. This may impact the use of wireless network access or email.

So it becomes important that your network provider deliver a secure transport of digital assets because a simple network is no longer adequate. The asset owner determines which data is subject to the restrictions, where in the infrastructure it resides, who accesses it, etc. Once this is defined, outside consultants and perhaps IT have a better chance of delivering the capability to meet the asset owner's demands. Neither data users nor data administrators are liable for failing to interpret the laws correctly, nor should they be.

Data administrators, at each stage of the ILM, must now provide the data users with the technology and best practices that comply with the concepts of due care. When this is properly done, regardless of pending regulations, at an infrastructure level, your data should be covered (unless there are specific infrastructure-related compliance stipulations).

ILM provides an easy-to-remember framework for developing security at every stage of data's life cycle.

Principle #3: The Power of Policy

Policy drives architecture and limits liability. Most companies seem to have a policy, but it often has little meaning to the organization. The power to limit liability lies in the enforcement and consistency of the policy. When a due-care issue arises or a violation occurs, the policy must be there to address it.

Earlier I discussed the employee who left a company laptop in his car which was then stolen. The company reported the laptop as stolen, but stated it was the result of an employee who broke policy and left the records unattended. In other words, the company claimed it was not liable for any damages resulting from data ending up in the wrong hands. It was a violation of policy.

Was the employee at fault, or was the company negligent?

If a case, such as this one, led to legal action, the employee would have to prove that the policy was actually a recommendation—not a formal policy. He can do this by showing that other policies have not been enforced and were treated as recommendations. If he's successful, the court may rule the policy was merely a recommendation, and the company would be liable for the loss. This is why it's so important to actually use and enforce company policy.

> **Policy drives architecture and limits liability.**

Compliance Is Driving Policy Changes

The link between policy and compliance is simple: As compliance areas are addressed, companies are changing policy to limit liability. Policy drives architecture. It's critical that the asset owner become involved in policy changes, and that data users and administrators are required to learn these new policies.

As I work with companies on policies, I find the standards often call for specific products, brands or industry certifications. If your company is going to develop these standards, data administrators must have a detailed understanding of the data they are working with, its value, and the types of attacks likely to target it. Technology is then chosen to help in securing data. But as we have seen, technology alone will not enforce the policy. The data user's understanding and threat awareness will be essential.

What Happens When Companies Fail to Comply?

Legally, this could lead to jail time, but more likely it will lead to fines, security breaches and loss of customer trust. What we *can* be sure of, based on history is this: If a company has a major security violation and loses significant data, it will have to prove it practiced due care. Management will have to show reasonable steps were taken to secure the data. Data owners may also have to demonstrate that their systems were in compliance with federal and industry regulations.

If we look at the last several years, fines have frequently come from the Federal Trade Commission. States such as California have laws that require companies operating within that state to disclose data theft to their customers when the data exposes personal information like account numbers or even a driver's license number. In 2007, VISA and MasterCard began developing an enforcement organization because they see the daily threat against their products. If credit card fraud continues to climb at the rates we are seeing, card usage, as we know it, could be at risk. Expect credit card companies to take action which will in turn move retailers to action.

Use All Three Principles to Leverage the Momentum Created by Compliance

While compliance itself has not moved every company to security, it has developed awareness among data owners. Corporate leaders are concerned with both company and personal liability, but don't focus on compliance itself. Instead, this should be delegated to your compliance officer or CSO. Focus on due care and the associated liability. Then, using the concepts of ILM, ask questions to discover digital assets and learn about the liabilities associated with data loss. This will help you understand your digital assets. Next, use policy to help limit liability while you promote an asset mindset among those in your company. Above all, remember Heartland and others who were supposedly PCI compliant, yet were compromised this year through the use of the tools I've discussed so far.

Dave Stelzl

Chapter 5

The Executive Guide to Understanding Security

Companies are spending more today on security than ever before and yet they are losing data. Do you know why? And is your security strategy as secure as you think?

Even if your security team is quiet, don't let your guard down. The methods and motives behind cybercrime have changed significantly over the past decade, which has dangerously lulled today's business leaders into a false sense of security.

During the development of identity focused cybercrime several years ago, I was tasked with running a national security practice that focused on network and system security. We were seeing exponential growth in the theft of information, and so were the companies we worked with.

Each day I contacted co-workers to ask what securities they would recommend for the projects they were overseeing. I was taken aback by their answers. They didn't view security as a priority and saw no need to secure the systems they were involved with. In fact, the lack of security-related disruptions had led them to believe computer crime was slowing.

I worked with an individual in South Carolina who was involved with a regional bank and worked with him on several initiatives. My job was to help educate our team about the need for security, so this seemed like a good place to start. He agreed to work with me and set up meetings to educate his clients about what I believed to be a growing urgency among companies nationwide, and even worldwide.

With three years of banking experience under my belt, I felt equipped to help this company understand the issue and build the right kind of security.

A week later, I was sitting in a meeting with three attendees from the bank, but all three were reluctant to hear about this urgent issue. The network administrator had come to defend the bank's current security product choices while the IT director was there to defend the employee's choices. The executive VP only put in an appearance but really didn't understand why he was needed at this technical meeting.

That's the first problem: security is often thought be a technical issue, but it isn't. So my challenge was helping them develop the asset mindset.

Security isn't a Technical Problem

In this chapter, we'll review the four key principles for developing security around an asset. These principles will build the foundation for asset owners and data users as they create and use assets. These same principles will apply to data administrators, helping them develop a framework for securing assets, not with technology, but with an asset mindset. Technology then helps automate and bring consistency to the security plan.

With the asset owner present in the bank meeting, I had an opportunity to help this company completely change the way they dealt with their assets. Now they could create a top-down approach to securing them and provide IT with the needed information to be successful in their mission. Part of this is bringing in the right technology to secure an asset they now understood.

This meeting turned into a win/win for everyone because they listened to my ideas. They agreed to assess their risk, whereas before management would not give IT approval for the assessment or get personally involved.

They had done assessments before, using security specialists from the outside that gave similar results each year. Generally the team walked through the building and provided a list of misconfigured systems, missing patches and a list of hardware and software required to make the system more secure. The reports were written in technical babble and were delivered to managers who generally turned them over to IT for deciphering.

This time the bank came to us, and we were leading with a different approach, developed and conducted along with the asset owner's involvement, but also with data users and IT involved. The process would measure actual risk rather than just check a bunch of patch levels, and the deliverable would be written with asset owners in mind.

Our unique methods produced a report that showed managers where the risk was, in their language, the level of risk and how to best secure the assets in question.

The State of Most Corporations

Going into that meeting, I needed to know what threats really existed, and how to discover threatened assets. First, it's realistic to assume ninety percent of the companies we see have inadequate security controls around a pivotal corporate asset: data.

Why? Mostly it is due to changes in attack methods against the security practices companies have been taught. It may be that security training has largely come from manufacturers of security products who have lead IT organizations down a path that will sell more of a given product. Meanwhile, it has completely avoided the involvement of senior managers – asset owners and data users.

This chapter will teach you how to understand the asset mindset approach to security and to discover where threats really exist, and why current security architectures are inadequate. As I alluded to earlier, it involves four key principles, starting with three simple questions.

Principles of Risk Management

Understanding security starts with understanding risk. The ability to manage risk is what data owners really want since it is the asset owner that is ultimately liable in the event of a security breach; they need to make sure company data is protected from misuse or theft.

There are several key areas of risk management that I use to develop the asset mindset – let's start by addressing some of the jargon. IT Security people especially need to understand that discussing security in some foreign vernacular is not helpful to the company.

AAA: To the technologist, AAA is just another three-letter acronym, treated almost as though it's a word. To the executive, it may be an automobile club. But talking about risk, it provides a structure for some very important questions.

1. Authorization: Providing data users with different levels of access privileges, including what they are allowed to see, change, create, delete, etc. who grants access, and at what levels? This must be established based on the sensitivity and value of the asset, which only the true asset owner knows.

2. Authentication: Identifying who's asking for data or network access is a critical area companies must control. The data administrator must have a way to determine if the people accessing the data are really the people who have been authorized. It is one thing to be authorized or given permission, and it's a much different thing to prove it is really you.

3. Accountability: This is the reporting mechanism that details who has accessed specific information, who gave employees access, when and what information was accessed, and what the data users did while accessing the data. Does IT have a way to identify what users are doing? Again, this is not technical, but rather driven by the asset owner.

MTD (Maximum Tolerable Downtime): How much downtime can you afford? Find out how important data is and how long the company can survive if it's unavailable. With every application it is critical that the data owners be involved in determining what is required by the business, and then have administrators and consultants that are able to deliver it. Since all this largely depends on technology, be careful when installing new systems or equipment.

RPO (Restore Point Objective): This is another storage term that focuses on how much data loss is acceptable. At what point must you be able to restore, and how much data can be lost between a backup and system failure? The answers given by data users and data owners tell the real story. Often this information is only made available to IT at the start of a new application or once data has been lost beyond acceptable levels.

CIA (Confidentiality, Integrity and Availability): Often considered the three pillars of security, each of these should be considered by the asset owner. Most of us think only of confidentiality or privacy of data, but the integrity and availability requirements are equally important in the security world and must be set by the asset owner.

Each of these topics is used to build a picture of risk in the minds of data users and data administrators. Risk is simply a look at impact versus likelihood:

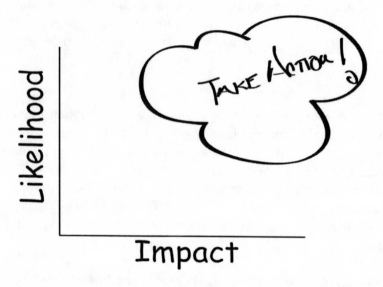

The concepts above provide a simplified framework for asking questions that uncover key assets, as well as the impact associated with losing confidentiality, availability and data integrity. If the impact is high, the issue is worth considering. The question is, what is the likelihood? Risk is really about making wise decisions and determining how likely it is that something will actually happen. We need to remember that our ability to predict an outcome is often tainted by appearances. In Las Vegas, games are made to look easy. There is always an advertisement displaying a couple that comes from an average lifestyle, holding a check for millions. But of course there are many rundown neighborhoods all over Las Vegas and the surrounding area. Meanwhile the hotels seem to have unlimited money to build and rebuild. It's clear that those who play and really think they will win are reading the risk factors incorrectly.

The same is true as IT security decisions are being made. What appears to be low risk may actually be very risky. At the same time, some perceived threats are very unlikely. For instance, it's not true that hackers are trying to break through your computer's firewall all the time. On the other hand, it sounds unlikely that someone will just call one of your administrative people for information, yet this is done successfully every day. So the question always comes back to, what is the impact if this data is compromised, and what is the likelihood? The ability to accurately predict this will go a long way in building the right security countermeasures. The truth is, malicious code is hitting your systems everyday through the open doors in your security strategy. Are you able to detect them?

When tragedy strikes an airline, risk managers have to consider the likelihood of whether the event will happen again. What are the chances that a plane will be sitting on the runway that's too short, while one person sits in air traffic control and gives the go-ahead to take off? Imagine that the pilots, unfamiliar with the airport, push their throttles forward and accelerate down the runway, only to find the strip is too short. Unlikely? You may remember an incident like this from 2006, and a tragedy resulted. So, what is the likelihood it will happen again? Is it high enough for someone to do something about it?

Your security plan should focus on likelihood and looking for the safeguards that may be used to reduce the chance of data being compromised. Some of this will be non-technical, such as dealing with who uses data, where, and how. At some point, technology will be used to automate and improve on the consistency of security around this data asset in question.

Layers of Security

When building a security strategy, the concept of security layers that work together to protect assets allows you to create security "in-depth." It doesn't make sense to buy a security product by itself, unless you're completing an already proven security strategy. Three types of controls must be considered:

1. Technical controls: Traditional security controls are firewalls, intrusion prevention software and passwords. Most companies will have at least a firewall in place and perhaps virtual private networking (VPN) technology. These alone will not protect data. They need to fit in with the rest of the security plan.

2. Physical controls: These include controlled access to wiring closets/data centers where devices can be compromised, security cameras or even security guards positioned in the lobby. Most companies will have some form of physical protection, but generally lack the security controls necessary to keep unauthorized users from accessing ports on computers in public-access locations. They also often assume that all insiders are trustworthy and that remote locations such as telecommuters and mobile systems don't count. Remember that these are two ways in which security fails.

3. Administrative controls: These are almost always inadequate. Kevin Mitnik in his book, *The Art of Deception*, reveals that the professional hacker starts by compromising systems that have poor administrative controls. This category includes security awareness training, security policies, disaster recovery and business continuity plans, and security and event correlation reports. Companies generally lack well-written, tested plans, and their policies are seldom maintained or enforced. The big hole is created because users have more access than they need, with less than adequate training on how to spot con artists looking for quick access. This is why training is important.

All three layers are required to build a sound security architecture. Most companies haven't thought them through in a consistent manner.

Four Foundational Principles of Asset Thinking

I used these four principles in my SC bank meeting so both the data administrator and the asset owner could understand what is happening in the security world. This is needed in order to provide asset owners and data users with the understanding they need to guard and use data safely. They can then use these principles to clarify this puzzle for others in their company.

Principle #1: Ask the Three Questions

The true asset owner has liability. Asset owners depend on this data for both their reputation and career, if the data is important. When highly sensitive data is lost, their picture may be on the front page, their reputation smeared, and they may be on a job hunt to replace their current salary, which could take months or even years.

Data users, however, might find themselves looking for a new position, and the same may be true of the data administrator, but the true liability falls on the data owner. However, whether you are really the asset owner or not, everyone needs this mindset when it comes to sensitive data. Everyone should see themselves as liable and willing to accept responsibility for their interaction with this asset.

So at the start of our meeting, when the IT team was eager to look at new technology, we began with three very non-technical questions, somewhat of a surprise to them. Turning to the asset owner, I asked these three questions:

Question 1: What are you trying to protect?

Question 2: What are the relevant threats?

Question 3: How comfortable are you with your organization's ability to detect, and respond to, a recognized threat before data is compromised?

Question 1: What are you trying to protect?

Your first objective is to move away from a technology meeting and focus on assets. The first question allows you to achieve this by concentrating your attention on mission-critical data.

The data owner's position on where risk exists is an essential starting point. This answer will take into consideration the company's use of the data, the data user's view of this data, and legal issues surrounding compliance and contracts. It may even change as company issues and internal politics influence the value of certain data.

I recently read an account where data, seemly innocuous, was backed up and sent off to a warehouse as usual. Nothing seemed improper here. Except in this case, this innocuous data was a critical factor in a legal battle regarding employee termination. The ex-employee in this story hired someone to track down this data by whatever means they might have at their disposal.

Using some questionable tactics, this group was able to con the warehouse operators into making a tape available to a newly added authorized person (added through some skilled social engineering). The data was used in court and the employee won. Only the asset owner could have known that this data was suddenly important. The company lost millions.

There are many acceptable answers to the question, "What are you trying to protect?" but "the network" isn't one of them. You're looking for data that exposes you to liability or places your company's reputation as a secure institution is in jeopardy. When I ask this question, I explain I'm looking for the items that would greatly impact the business if compromised or inaccessible. If the question is framed correctly, I expect dialogue on mission-critical systems. In my SC meeting, we spent the bulk of our meeting on this first question. At the end of our dialogue, I had a thorough understanding of the bank's key assets and the impact associated with loss or compromise. I had the bottom line of my risk graph.

Answers often include financial data, company secrets, pending patents, customer account numbers or key applications.

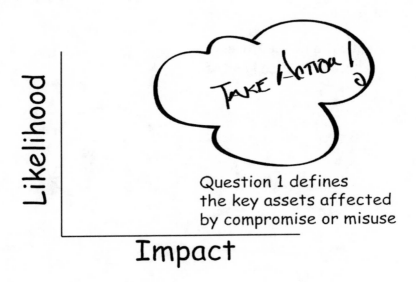

Question 1 defines
the key assets affected
by compromise or misuse

Question 2: What are the relevant threats?

Next, we must determine the likely threats. Understanding what threats will provide your company with a critical foundation for developing information security. Don't assume all companies are under the same threats or that small companies have no threats.

Asset owners, yourself included, may not be aware of all impending security threats. Finding out what threats are real—and most risky to the company—will be helpful in developing a relevant security plan.

Special issues such as laying off IT people, internal staff issues, use of various contractors or guest access, are going to be important considerations. This is a good time to consider any past security issues.

In my SC meeting, I developed a clear understanding of the likely threats this asset owner anticipated. This made part of the Y axis of my risk graph:

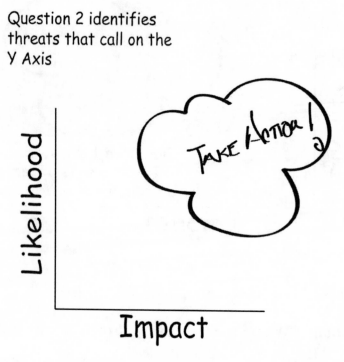

Question 2 identifies
threats that call on the
Y Axis

Likelihood

Take Action!

Impact

Question 3: How comfortable are you with your organization's ability to detect, and respond to, a recognized threat before data is compromised?

It is equally important to determine the asset owner's comfort level with his current security strategy. Most evaluations incorrectly assume that IT can answer these questions which can lead to poor security planning. In order for you, the asset owner, to drive the right security plan, all participants must understand the real threats. This comes from a clear understanding of the asset.

Are there competitors and thieves who want this data? Some education may be required here, but in the end, the asset owner must provide the answer to this question. This completes the risk, Impact vs. Likelihood graph from the asset owner's perspective.

The FBI, CIA, other government entities and many major U.S. banks have been hacked successfully in the last few years, so it's hard to believe anyone would feel "very" comfortable at this time. Micheal Santarchangelo, in his book, *Into the Breach*, tells us that companies with all "green lights" on their assessment ratings are going to be most vulnerable as they let down their guards.

In most cases, I expect asset owners to be unsure about the true state of their ability to defend their assets. They likely are not seeing any real evidence of danger even though, at some point, they may report a security breach. This is a result of the computer industry making security a purely technical issue.

So now the picture should be complete with an understanding of the asset owner's key assets, top known threats, priority of systems and comfort level. The initial risk graph is now established.

Next we consider the organization's approach to security, explaining how security works and why most systems are likely less secure than the organization thinks.

Principle #2: How Security Works

The three questions identify assets and risk. They allow you to build the risk, impact vs. likelihood graph, providing a clear picture of where the focus needs to be. Your next goal is to understand how any security architecture must operate. Many companies I visit have not thought this through. Instead they have bought various technologies over time that sounded good, then constructed a disjointed strategy they call security. My bank meeting was really no different. Working with the asset owner, we used this simple house model to create an understanding of how security actually works. Not a set of products, not even a network, but just straight forward security.

An analogy of a house, a physical structure we like to consider safe, works because it represents security that in general does work. The same can be said for your office building, the bank you use, or any other physical location you consider to be somewhat safe.

After drawing a simple house on a whiteboard, I asked the asset owner to share how he secures his house. During this brainstorming exercise, he identified a list of obvious structures and programs seen in most homes or buildings. Together we created a simple chart that looks something like this:

Doors	Alarm	Dog
Locks	Motion detector	Gun
Windows	Monitoring	Police
Fence	Crime watch	Insurance

I then divided this list into three columns, asking him to help me categorize his lists. Notice that I grouped the items in a particular order, regardless of how they were given to me.

1.	2.	3.
Doors	Alarm	Dog
Locks	Motion detector	Gun
Windows	Monitoring	Police
Fence	Crime watch	Insurance

What criteria were used for each list? At first glance, people usually guessed that the first column applies to a home's physical features. But if you look again, you'll see they are all physical.

I refer to Column 1 as my proactive protection column. Once Column 1 is labeled, it is easy to conclude that the second column is about detection, while Column 3 applies to response.

This is my PDR Model: protection, detection, response. Every security architecture in the world (that works) is based on these three pillars.

There is a barrier set in place or a policy that must not be violated. Once crossed or broken, a detection mechanism kicks in and alerts the waiting response. If any one of these columns fails, the security program will not work. It's a fairly simple model that has been used for thousands of years.

The important question is: "Which column is most critical to security?" In other words, which one must you have the greatest focus on?

Well, it's obvious to most people that Column 1: Protection, will be the one to focus on, if it works. The idea is to keep out the trouble and nothing else will matter. While this is theoretically true, security architecture has always relied more on Column 2 to secure assets. Here's why: Sitting in that bank meeting, I asked my client if his doors were open. He replied yes. I then asked if his vault was open. Again he responded with a nod. This is almost always true as verified at a recent banker's association meeting where I gave a similar keynote.

"So, what is protecting the money?" I asked. There are many layers of security in a bank. Cameras and security guards observe activity throughout the day. If someone violates policy by stepping behind the teller line, drawing a weapon or wandering down the wrong hallway, a well-timed response plan will kick in. And how about at night? The doors are locked, but could easily be broken through if crooks don't care about the threat of the alarm system. So it's not the initial protection, but rather detecting realized threats that will provide security.

One's house, too, has no real security without detection. The idea that your doors will deter a determined intruder is clearly wrong thinking. Can you recall shopping for a door or window if you have ever built a house? Did you and your spouse look for the most secure door, or was it the mahogany door with the decorative windows on the side that caught your eye? Likely the latter – the one that provides the easy to crack side windows for instant access to the bolt. On the other hand, when you picked out your alarm system, I doubt that you were looking for the most decorative unit. No, you likely read consumer reports to find out which was the most effective and fail safe.

Once detected, a well time response plan is required to complete the program.

Again, the point of these comparisons is to step back from technology and look at examples of security that work—to demonstrate three critical aspects to security architecture that show the detection process is vital to asset protection.

Of course it would be wrong to assume that protection is not needed. Remember I said that all three categories must work together.

Principle# 3: It's Easy to Get in

Once we understand the power of detection and its important role in the security model, it's time to illustrate how easily one can infiltrate a company's network. I like to draw a simple two-cloud network, showing the internal network and the Internet so we can see how a bot network (botnet) is established.

The top cloud represents the insecure Internet, including remote users as well as cyberthieves looking to steal data. The bottom cloud, the secure corporate network, connects to the top cloud, delivering customer facing applications, allowing data users to access outside resources such as Internet email and providing connectivity to the world. The assumption is that all corporate data is behind a corporate protective shield we call the perimeter. Of course this is a false sense of security. Your data is everywhere, and many of your data users are outside the boundaries of your "secure" network.

With a bit of social engineering, combined with amazing technology, getting past the firewall is so simple that just about any teenager, competitor, or unfriendly country, will quickly gain access to what they want.

People love to receive email. And no matter how many times they're told, "Don't open that email," they continue to do it. There are many roads into a network, including email, instant messaging (IM), Really Simple Syndication (RSS) and websites. The most basic music, video and picture downloads can be used to infect systems. Certainly more than half the spam out there is infected.

If I were an attacker, all I would need to do is convince the recipient to click on a link or open a file, allowing me to install malware on a system. To access the entire company system, I need just one employee out of the hundreds or thousands to click my link. Firewalls don't stop many of the threats used by organized crime in this information-theft era.

In most cases, there is no real hacking required. Remember the social engineering tactics I   referred to earlier. Here's how it works:

Bob: "Hi Mary, I'm from IT in the Charlotte Branch. We have been receiving reports that some of the Corporate Lending folks are having network problems. Are you seeing anything like that on your end?"

Mary: "No, everything seems to be up and running, perhaps a little slow, but that's usual around here."

Bob: "Great, I just wanted to make sure. I'm checking with some of the different department administrators to make sure we don't experience downtime where we don't have to. Say, Mary, while I have you on the phone, do you think you could just check one thing for me?"

Mary: "Sure, I guess I have a minute."

Bob: "Great, this will just take a minute…"

After having Mary check a few technical items in areas she is not familiar with, he walks her through downloading a simple patch from www.banksupport.com. Once downloaded, Mary should be all set and they hang up.

Later that evening, Bob is able to access Mary's computer remotely, setting up password logging tools and a root kit that will allow him complete control of the system and access to any passwords. Bob has successfully gained information from the corporate external website, learned the names of company locations, made a few calls to figure out where Mary is located and has convinced her with little difficulty that he is the IT support person. By proactively helping her avoid downtime, he has instantly created an ally. Likely he can continue to call on Mary to gather even more information as time goes on.

But there is more. What about online resumes? This may seem like more innocuous information, but it's not when we consider it from the asset mindset. How much information are people in your organization giving away to people like Bob on resumes? It might be educational to go out and look at some online resumes. Every system, operating system, network architecture, and even security system is likely listed once you compile the many online resumes submitted by people that work for your company. This gives the hacker everything they need to talk to Mary like they own the place. It also provides contacts of people who might be willing to work on the side, helping intruders for a fee. Studies show that organized crime will pay significant salaries to insiders for laundering money, changing log files on computers, installing remote control software or perhaps just looking the other way.

It is easy to break in. Anyone who really wants to can.

Protection Alone will not Protect - Why You Need Detection

Companies may have some intrusion prevention software running at the perimeter, but the ability to detect and respond to attacks throughout the computing environment is generally quite weak. Most companies will be unable to detect and respond to attacks coming from wireless networks, remote access, compromised laptops, Bluetooth technology and the like. And this is no surprise. When security was deemed a technical problem, companies looked to technology to solve the problem, and firewalls came to the rescue. Somewhere around 1995, companies developed stateful inspection firewalls with the claim that they could not be hacked. Of course, as we can see from the above illustrations, no hacking is needed.

The asset mindset recognizes that technology has provided something that worked 10 years ago: the idea that a firewall would protect the internal network from Internet threats and that a password would do the rest. If security is going to work, everyone who touches data (asset owners, data users, and data administrators) must come to an understanding – detection is generally missing, but quite essential.

To solidify the point, consider Column 1 of the house model. What would you have to do to secure the house through Column 1? Some military facilities rely heavily on Column 1, yet those in charge understand it's not enough. With a house, you'd need to spend hundreds of thousands of dollars—and even into the millions—to create a perfectly safe home without relying on detection schemes – and still it wouldn't really work. Can the homeowner really build a castle with insurmountable walls, moats and razor wire?

All that protection is completely "over the top" and unnecessary when you realize it costs about $30 a month to hire a security monitoring company, with alarm equipment included. It becomes clear, with proper analysis, that **detection - response** is a key part of any security strategy—and in most cases technology companies have failed to bring this strategy to corporate America.

Principle #4 –The Holistic Security Model

Finally, the asset mindset depends on a holistic security model. I call this table "The Coverage Model." It gives the asset owner a better understanding of how security done properly will defend corporate assets.

	Protection	Detection	Response
Admin	Policy		Business continuity plan
Tech		Intrusion prevention software	
Physical		Checking badges	Guards

It's a simple three-by-three grid, taking the concepts from the house illustration—protection, detection and response—and combining them with three basic types of security controls (administrative, technical, and physical). Don't worry about filling in the entire table right now; instead, consider how these nine boxes provide a comprehensive approach to securing data. If your company treats these boxes as silos or is spending the greatest efforts on just one or two, your security model won't stand the test.

The asset mindset must view these as integrated controls that work together through the infrastructure and organization to enable a strong security architecture. Only then can pieces be delegated to technicians, policies, procedures and technology.

Using this diagram, it becomes clear: It's not a firewall problem anymore. As you can see, these issues have little to do with firewalls and brute-force hacking. Security is a matter of assets and risk, the likely threats and their ultimate impact.

At this point you may be asking whether security, following this approach, will prevent hackers from breaking in. My response: "No, I guarantee they will break in. The question is, will you be able to detect and respond before your assets are compromised?"

Remember, this approach is holistic and uses not only protection, but detection and response.

Bringing These Four Principles Together

If you come from the technical side, you may be saying, "This model is pretty basic, what's the big deal?" The big deal is that, while this seems obvious, most companies don't have the asset owners involved, have not created proper awareness among data users, and have not developed a strategy that really allows detection to take place across the company.

Having presented this in board meetings, executive-level association meetings, keynotes, and on a napkin at dinner, I can safely say that most asset owners have not really considered this and found it eye opening at the least.

But it's not the house that matters; it's the key principles:

The three questions move our thinking away from technology and onto the assets. It forces data owners, users, and administrators to look at data assets together and from each other's perspective.

If you are going to build a corporate-wide asset mindset, each person must understand the assets they have access to and how detection works; **the House** model demonstrates this. Culturally this will mean that users are aware, understand security violations, and know what to do when they see one. More often than not, detection is going to mean detecting violations of policy such as taking data where it should not go – home on laptops and home PCs.

The **Cloud** demonstrates how easy it is to break in, and that firewalls do not stop hackers. Firewalls are just one of the nine boxes, contributing to the overall security model. All nine are required and must work together.

The **Coverage Model**: everyone must agree that this is not a technical issue that should be delegated completely to the IT department. Asset protection requires holistic thinking around products, policies, procedures and education. It's a big issue and data owners, users and administrators will work together to create a more secure computing environment.

Security Sinkholes

So what if your security program really is solid? The truth is, some companies think they have it covered. This thinking may be coming from senior management or it may come from IT, but regardless of where it comes from it is wrong, especially when you consider the power of social engineering. Let's face it, if the Pentagon can be breached (and Department Of Defense reports indicate that this has been a frequent occurrence) so can your company. Especially if someone working with organized crime can find an unhappy employee willing to take a bribe.

For the company that has done everything reasonable to secure its data, I refer you to my trusty security sinkhole list—a compilation of the areas almost always lacking in due care:

- Compliance
- Policy and liability
- Perimeter
- Wi-Fi
- Identity management
- Remote access
- Information life-cycle
- Applications
- Business continuity and disaster recovery plan
- Messaging
- Mobility/Connectivity
- Untrained people with access

In particular, areas like remote access, wireless, user awareness and application security are severely lacking. The perimeter may have most of what is needed, but when we start moving to these other areas, I find networks and systems to be very insecure.

By 2008 more than 650 major organizations reported losing identity information, exposing more than 200 identities according to national news sources. It would be foolish for someone to feel completely secure, given the news we read every day. Bottom line, it scares me when I hear someone say, "We've got it covered."

Asset Owners and the Security Team

Remember: Security is about protecting assets. It should be implemented by Asset Owners, Data Users, IT, Security consultants, and anyone who touches the data. It can then be managed and maintained by those appointed to various aspects of the coverage model. This may include departmental points of contact, IT, a managed services group you contract with, or a security boutique firm you work with. Some of this will be automated through technology, but some will be policy driven, requiring an ongoing user training and awareness program. Keep it interesting, short, and frequent to get people thinking daily about security.

Part Two

Dave Stelzl

Chapter 6

Mindset #1: Asset Aware

Security is an Asset issue. When security is seen only as a technical issue, too much responsibility falls on data administrators, a group destined to fail without the direction and support of the data owners and users.

The asset owner is in the best position to know data's value, instruct others on its sensitivity and keep the organization focused on relevant threats, yet they are often least equipped to secure it. With this in mind we begin with the first and most basic of the seven mindsets: being asset aware.

The Asset Aware mindset starts with the asset owner. However, it is equally important that data users and data administrators consider and learn this mindset. Why? The asset owner generally knows what is in the data they create and use. This person is also generally liable if it gets placed in the hands of the wrong people or its integrity is compromised, making future use impossible or expensive. Availability may also be in jeopardy if the proper infrastructure is not built to support this data. End users and administrators may simply see information as data, a necessary part of the job, but have no sense of urgency to keep it secure. The IT organization may simply protect it within whatever budget is available, regardless of the security required, while end-users focus only on job efficiency which may at times place these assets in jeopardy.

The Technologist Mindset vs. Asset Mindset

Data security shouldn't be left just to a technologist operating in the IT organization. IT is often appointed to support applications, provide connectivity, provide access to data users, and ensure that data is not lost, misused or stolen.

What IT is not given are instructions on the changing value and the threat landscape surrounding this data. I once worked with a team of web application providers who were part of a global technology provider organization. I was building a security team under the umbrella of this organization with the goal of creating more secure applications. It wasn't long before management moved our security group to the infrastructure side of the business because the applications people wanted little to do with our assessments, controls and risk oriented thinking. Securing applications was seen as inhibiting sales since this made the application more expensive, cumbersome to use, and raised too many issues in the eyes of our potential customers. In the end, this entire group just wanted to sell their applications and leave security to a future project, handled by some other group.

This same problem often occurs on the infrastructure side as well; I call this the Technologist Mindset.

The Asset Mindset	The Technologist Mindset
Values the Business	Values Their Position
Understands Asset Value	Hardware and Application Centered
Sense of liability	Fascinated by New Attacks
Process innovation	Technology Frontiers and Knowledge
Business growth	Empire Building
Operational efficiency	Job Security Through Complexity
Return on investment	Wants New Technology
Risk mitigation	Gaining experience

This isn't to say the Technologist Mindset is the dominant way of thinking in all IT people; in fact, companies that are doing an effective job with security are inherently working with an *asset*.

In the table above, I have identified seven important distinctions between the two mindsets. Let's discuss these seven aspects so everyone that touches company data, either as a user or as an administrator, will understand the asset mindset.

Values Business vs. Values Position: Asset owners are generally people working on the profit center side of the business. They run departments, hire knowledge workers, and find new ways to generate business or grow the business. They are particularly focused on creating a part of the business that will grow over time and gain value to the company overall. These roles often include executive management, line of business management, and other leadership positions within the company.

While their position is important to them, if they have an asset mindset they value the company and their department to the point where they feel personal responsibility for the profitability and performance of their group. As an aside, there may be people in these roles that don't actually have an asset mindset. When this is true, company leadership should consider replacing them with someone who cares about the company as well as their position. As well known speaker, Alan Weiss, says in his leadership seminar, "Leaders lead out front, and leaders take the blame."

It can be a temptation to have the technologist mindset in many support functions as well. The same is true for non-technical roles, just under another name. I use the term technologist here in a broad sense, as does Michael Gerber in his book e-*Myth Revisited*. Gerber really clarifies these roles when he compares the technologist to the entrepreneur, saying the technical mindset is one that just performs a function in the business rather than watching over the business.

In my distinction, the technologist mindset is more focused on the mechanics of their job, thinking about what will strengthen their role in the company, create more job stability and build a stronger resume. InformationWeek's 2007 job survey, cited earlier in the book, reveals that many technicians are there just to do their job, not to build the company. By the way, this is not only true for IT workers. Steven Covey, in his book *The Eight Habits*, draws similar conclusions about departmental workers. With this in mind, both data users and administrators must be encouraged to adopt an asset mindset as long as they have access to critical corporate data. (It helps to be a company that values its employees, which is the topic of numerous books.)

"All I need now is a VOIP server to complete my cubical area network (CAN)!"

Understanding Asset Value vs. Hardware and Applications: To the asset owner, technology is the plumbing. When they can't get to their Enterprise Resource Planning (ERP) application, we hear, "ERP is down." The technologist answers back, "ERP is up, it's the network, stupid."

To the asset minded person, the value of the data is the primary consideration. Budgets are approved based on the value and importance of data and applications. Responsible executives are not approving new technology expenditures based on the cool factor of new technology. They consider Return on investment (ROI), operational efficiency and risk factors that might upset the business.

Assets are created with some known value, and while this value is probably not passed down to the technology support people, the asset owner knows. It may be the thing that makes your company a candidate for Jim Collin's next edition of *Good to Great*. Over time the value of your data will change. The asset mindset is watching these factors and acting accordingly. Meanwhile the technical mindset is just watching to make sure the network is up and running, applications are properly executing, and backups are taking place. It's all part of the job, and in general, all data is made of bits and bytes. Administrators of data must differentiate; they must consider the asset's changing value.

Remember the manager in London who handed one of their employees a CD containing important information to be delivered to one of the end-user departments? They lost this data simply because they did not have an asset mindset. They were not aware of the asset, and then the package never showed up at its destination even though we believe the envelope was properly addressed. Because the manager was not thinking about the assets, and handed them to the administrative person, who also was not thinking about the assets, the data disappeared.

A Sense of Liability vs. Fascination with New Attacks: Liability is most often associated with the asset owner. Both data users and data administrators are largely free from liability, unless of course they perform some illegal activity as we have seen numerous times since the Enron case.

When I say liability, I mean the kind of liability that could threaten someone's long term career or livelihood. When I bring this up, I frequently hear a groan from the technical side of the house – "We absolutely do have liability," they say. I would agree that higher up in the organization; CFOs, CIOs and other CXO positions are liable.

If data is stolen, it isn't the IT administrator's picture that will end up in the paper. This person may get ousted for political reasons, but in the end it will all work out. There is a shortage of strong IT candidates out there, and this new level of security experience gained through a recent security breach is sure to land them a better job, but not the asset owner. This sobering fact reminds asset owners why they shouldn't just "delegate" security to IT .

Process Innovation vs. Technology Frontiers: As we said, asset owners frequently fall either on the profit center side of the organization or are part of the executive management team. As an innovator in your business, you are working hard to increase the value you bring to the organization. Building a mindset toward enhancing company valuation requires both IT and asset owners to understand the value of data and apply technology to the business in a business centric way. This involves aligning IT with the business.

On the other hand, the technology mindset continues to build complexity into the computing environment, looking at new technology, new learning opportunities and personal resume building. Conversely, IT people that work to bring profitable innovation to the organization are demonstrating an asset mindset and should be rewarded.

Business Growth vs. Empire Building: With complexity comes the demand for resources, both technical and human. While the asset mindset seeks to grow the business, profit, financial growth, and market strength, the technical mindset is building an empire, asking for more resources, more equipment, and more office space. Often decisions are made at the expense of the company placing emphasis on growing the empire, not making security more efficient.

Operational Efficiency vs. Job Security Through complexity: Earlier in my career I was managing the IT team for a large bank. I remember bringing in an influx of programmers through an acquisition made in Texas one year. The bank merger process was in full swing, bringing new geographies, new executives, new ideas and a host of new technologists. Our model had been pretty straight forward up until then. Among other improvements, we were setting up PCs with Windows on every desktop. We had programmers, but they were dedicated to customer banking applications used for functions run on midrange and mainframe systems.

To our surprise, the acquired company staffed numerous programmers that were learning to customize the Microsoft Windows environment. I can understand why a bank would staff programmers to create special applications not available through third-party ISVs (Independent Software Vendors), but these people were there to customize the basic Windows interface. This added all kinds of complexity to the boot up process, the interface, adding menus and icons that were done with such complexity that no one was able to support the desktop environment without their help.

Documentation was not part of their offering, so they were establishing their own job security by making the computing environment more complex, without contributing much to the overall functionality of the system. This is a wrong mindset.

Return on Investment vs. Wanting new Technology: The asset owner is concerned with bottom-line profits, shareholder value and the growing competitive advantage of the company. This mindset makes decisions that offer some return on investment over some period of time. Opposing this cost saving mindset is one that continually evaluates technology and seeks approval, not with the intent of expanding the business but simply to create new learning experiences, demand more resources, and add value to a growing resume. If IT is going to secure data, they must understand what is valuable to the organization, where profits are earned, and where investments should be made.

Risk Mitigation vs. Technology Experience: The asset mindset is looking to avoid loss and minimize risk. Steps are taken to identify procedures within the department, new people are often trained to do things a certain way, and technology is purchased to help conduct business in a secure manner. But over time these principles are often lost. The technology mindset takes over as IT is given the task of setting up new users and providing access to applications and associated data.

Asset awareness is required here. The technologist mindset is to find new technologies to introduce into the organization without taking into consideration the company's best interest. In fact, less secure choices may be made simply because there are divided responsibilities within supporting departments such as IT, telecom, and perhaps security, and they all want to maintain technology within their jurisdiction. This always complicates the end product and results in a less secure solution. Becoming asset aware is absolutely an IT issue that is frequently left out of the job description.

A Data User's First Concern – Getting the Job Done

The asset aware mindset is something the data owner likely has, but equally important is building this mindset into the daily lives of data users.

Data users are the knowledge workers in any given department that create and use data on a daily basis, have more access privileges than just about any person in the company (outside of IT) and may carry more authority in demanding certain levels of access. And yet they possess the least amount of knowledge when it comes to data value to outsiders and a clear understanding when it comes to threats and security risk. For good reasons, data users are known for wanting to get the job done.

Data users are managed by other data users or perhaps report right to a data owner – both are looking for results. They have deadlines to meet, frequently work for profit center areas of the company, and are paid for their ability to deliver goods and services to the end-customer.

This is where cyber-crime often starts. Professional hackers call data users and administrative people working for data owners. They user clever tactics from thorough research to convince data users that they work for the company or for a trusted third-party processor, one that would normally have access at some level to the assets we are considering.

Building the asset aware mindset is critical in securing data. Anyone who has access to sensitive data must:

- Understand the policies and procedures that govern data,
- Know what a violation looks like when they see one,
- Know what to do about it,
- And be willing to take action.

In part three of this book I spend some time on user awareness and how to create an effective user awareness program. This must become an ongoing initiative among data users, making them aware of the changing value and the relevant threats associated with the data they access.

They must also be willing to accept a "need to know" policy for data access. Rather than demanding they have full access to all the data they could possibly need, they must accept the policies that require oversight and accountability, and be willing to involve others when requiring special information. Remember, this group is likely the weakest link in your company's security program.

Where Compromises Occur

Often the most important data is thought to be well guarded, but it is the innocuous data that professional hackers use to gain access to the real secrets buried deep within the company. Familiarity with a company and its internal language, locations, procedures and culture allows unauthorized criminals to appear authorized. What information do you publish that might be used in this way?

Take a look at your corporate website. Knowing your locations, personnel listed, email addressing schemes and product set provides a good start to criminals. Of course some of these things need to be advertised, but add less available data such as online resumes that contain the details of your operating systems, applications, security products and even patch levels. It would not be uncommon for a technical person to list the exact computing platforms they work on with the operating system levels and even the types of security products they work with.

Creating the Asset Mindset

Being asset aware is simply a mindset that understands that all data is an asset at some level. When assets are created they should be classified, associated with corporate policy, and awareness of the asset should be passed on to all parties involved, mainly the data users and data administrators.

Elements of the Asset Mindset

The essential elements of being asset aware are simply this:

- **An awareness of what you are trying to protect.** The questions owners, users and administrators should be asking - **what assets matter to the company?** Answers will vary over the lifecycle of data so people should constantly ask the question. The answer provides us with a list of assets and their relative value to the organization.

- **Knowing the relative threats.** Threats change and are growing in number and sophistication as thieves learn to capitalize on stolen information.
- **How comfortable are you with your organization's ability to detect and respond?** This last question should be top of mind for all asset owners. There are two considerations here: first, are the data users aware and do they recognize there is a problem? Secondly, does IT have the checks and balances in place to deal with a compromise? Can they detect a breach and respond before it's too late?

The Role of the Chief Security Officer (CSO)

Larger companies will have an officer level executive responsible for IT security, smaller companies likely will not. In either case, someone must be overseeing this asset. I recently had a conversation with a CSO overseeing a large operation in the hospitality vertical. After attending one of my seminars, he was frustrated with the lack of support he was receiving from other executives in the organization. In their opinion, it was his responsibility to secure data, and this should be done by working with IT to apply the proper security technology. We immediately set a date for me to present to them on user awareness. The asset aware mindset needs to be part of the organization's culture.

CSOs can't secure data. They can bring awareness programs to the data users, they can understand the value of the assets a company uses to conduct business, and they can help create and maintain the policies and procedures that allow a company to operate without excessive exposure. Their role is to create the vision and lead the team through a well defined plan, but left alone, they don't have the support of the organization and cannot fulfill their calling.

Educating the Organization

Education has to start at the top. Everything depends on the value of the assets a company is creating and using. Once values are known, classification schemes can be used to communicate asset value to those who use and access or administer the systems housing the data. Some thoughts on creating an asset aware mindset include:

1. Involving data owners in the communication process to data users.
2. Developing accountability for the use and access involving highly sensitive data.
3. Requiring users to read and sign off on policies.
4. Appointing departmental level people to help maintain policies.

The important thing here is to be aware of the assets that exist, those that are being created, and those that may be sought after. In the coming mindsets we'll talk about being digitally aware, which is a similar concept. But first, we will address the need to create a restrictive mindset, one that keeps watch over who is in possession or has access to these critical or sensitive assets.

Chapter 7

Mindset #2: Restrictive

Who has your data? Do you think of those you are hiring as data users? They change jobs, take on new responsibilities and at some point move on to new companies or departments. Who is maintaining the proper level of access for these individuals, and what about mobile users, telecommuters and contractors? Do you know where your data is?

In addition to being asset aware, you need to know where your data is and who touches it. I call this the restrictive mindset because asset owners must require some level of accountability when others are accessing these assets. It seems that consultants always come back with a list of dormant accounts, and my firm finds that people are taking data and sending data to unsecure places and using it in unsecure ways.

Asset owners generally know the data they create and use, and as the person liable when it is compromised, the asset owner should be in control of it. Availability is something asset owners must also be aware of, and if the proper infrastructure is in place to support this asset. In this chapter we will take a look at areas where asset owners tend to lose control, and then I'll provide steps to getting everyone on board with a new level of accountability.

Data Users: the Weak Link

Security is only a good as the weakest link. The best technology in the world cannot defend against a good social engineer because social engineering methods attack data users who don't understand the value of the data they access. From there, hackers can use all kinds of technology to take control of the assets you are liable for.

Home Computers

At the end of the day, data users need to go home and tend to family matters, yet the work often isn't done. So they copy the needed data to a portable device or email it to an unsecure account in order to access it from their home system. At the same time, their children are finishing up hours of online video games and social site interaction, not to mention downloads of their favorite movies and videos. When work and home life meet on the computer, bad things start happening. It won't be obvious , but more than half of the downloads family members are accessing contain malware that will go undetected by most antivirus software programs. While it seems like no one would want to access your personal system, automation has made you and your data users targets at home. Just think of how many people get and open a certain spam email.

Employees finish their work at home and give little thought to who else might have access to that computer. It may be spyware, or it may be the neighbor sharing an insecure wireless network. Most data users don't understand enough about technology to lock these home systems down, and of course IT doesn't have jurisdiction here. So the computer is operating in an insecure state, open to whoever might find it. Even if wireless networks are using some level of encryption, most are easily broken into. If that doesn't happen, web browsers will hit infected websites and downloads. Home systems are just not safe places to work with sensitive material unless the user really understands security at some level.

Traveling Computers

Then there's laptop computers used by traveling employees at home and on the road, filled with countless files of sensitive data. As I mentioned earlier, luggage tags are often enough to entice anyone looking for data. If the hacker is lucky, it'll even have a note with the VPN access codes on it; all the software needed to log in and the stored passwords. Since the user is traveling, they have downloaded all necessary data from the mainframe or servers, and of course the computer will contain the data from past trips since no one ever deletes anything.

"Phishing"

Peer to Peer Networks and Internet Music

Perhaps one of the least understood issues when considering the **Restrictive Mindset** is just how vulnerable users are when working at home or remotely. Employees may see policies against certain data handling as overbearing or too restrictive. Everyone from executives to data users and administrators likely use peer to peer networks for music and video sharing or maybe they have family members that do.

An explanation of peer to peer, or P2P, networks will show why they are so dangerous to corporate data, and this is quickly becoming one of the most widely used applications on the Internet. P2P networks are set up by downloading free software that will turn your local computer or laptop into an Internet server which others can then search from any internet connection. The benefits are both corporate and personal. People use this technology to exchange everything from music and videos to corporate documents they may be collaborating on (something that should not be done).

Communications are set up between your system and millions of other personal computers on the Internet, advertising the files you made available. You get to see music from millions of users right on their hard drive, and you can click on them to download them to your computer. In addition to copyright violations, there are many risks in doing this.

Is Your System a Part of a P2P Network?

Just because you haven't downloaded P2P software doesn't mean you are not on the network and part of the sharing group. Many of the computers out there are added by kids who use their parent's work computers, with or without permission. The installation process is pretty simple and default options are used if you don't select something different. Given the amount of corporate information available on P2P networks today, it looks like many are accepting the default settings and sharing their entire documents folder, containing all of your personal and office work.

Examples of P2P clients include Kazaa, Morpheus Soulseek and many more. These applications access P2P networks that may go by the names of BitTorrent or Gnutella. You might want to do a quick search of your applications to see if your system has any of these names installed on it.

Corporate Exposure

In 2008 Pfizer was investigated after the personal data of 17,000 current and former employees was leaked over the Internet, according to reports in InformationWeek magazine. It turned out that *one* employee's family member had installed P2P software on a company laptop to share music or videos. Along with sharing their music files, they shared 2300 company files containing everything from Social Security Numbers, addresses, salary information and names. All this was openly shared with no access control restrictions.

In 2007 we saw similar reports from Amro Mortgage Group. Files containing the personal data of 5000 of its customers were made available through P2P software running on an employee's computer. Results from a study conducted by an analyst from the University of Florida's Health Science Center showed that, after installing P2P software and a few search tools, the analyst was able to find hundreds of business related documents including spreadsheets, billing data, health records, RFPs, audit reports, product specifications and a host of other sensitive looking documents.

This type of exposure may be far worse than losing a laptop. Lost hardware, in the hands of one person who may or may not want the data, presents a problem. Hopefully they are more interested in selling the hardware on eBay or a pawn shop, making this more of an inconvenience than data exposure. (Of course, someone might buy the laptop from a pawn shop looking for data.) Conversely, when files are advertised online through P2P networks, they become searchable to any other P2P user. Files will be easily found by groups using automated search engines targeting this type of data, and this data is downloaded without you ever knowing about it. After all, that's the point of P2P. Once taken, hackers may post your data on P2P servers all over the world. At this point, there is no recovering the data. It's now public information.

One analyst report gives details of how P2P software was used to discover hundreds of files by searching for SSN (Social Security numbers). Continuing on, he was able to find a file that contained dozens of online banking passwords, Equifax credit reports and even tax returns. He even found what P2P networks refer to as an information concentrator, an aggregator of information generally used by thieves who are collecting and storing information to steal identities. He goes on to show his discoveries of insider political information, home phone numbers and cell phone numbers of political figures, their meeting notes, fund-raising plans, and various confidential documents including medical records, some of which contained incriminating reports of HIV.

In another study conducted by Tiversa, and company that provides services to help protect against P2P leaks, they collected 114,000 bank related files. One spreadsheet in this find included 23,000 business bank accounts including names, titles, addresses and account numbers.

Who is looking at your data?

Make no mistake, data thieves are well aware that this is happening. While some of the larger companies have taken steps to stop P2P networks, the problem continues to grow. Most corporate security is limited to the physical office location. Once a user heads out on a trip or goes to their home office, unless IT has taken special steps of action, they are going to be on insecure networks where there is little restriction. This problem is exacerbated when users email data to insecure home systems or carry portable media that will later be used on personal or home systems.

Once thieves have found you, anything contained in shared folders (something you or your family member set up during the initial install) will be shared without restriction. Data thieves then set up concentrators as mentioned above, which automatically search P2P networks looking for file names that sound like confidential or financial information. In 2007 Seattle authorities arrested one man who had amassed thousands of tax return files, financial aid applications, credit reports and account information which he then used to set up credit cards and loans fraudulently, according to one report I read.

Stopping the Problem

Stopping this is not going to be easy. Once laptops or mobile data leave the office, your control is limited. The first steps include:

1. Educating data owners, data users and data administrators of the dangers associated with P2P networks. This does not mean that all P2P networking needs to stop. In fact you won't be able to stop it, but people who touch data must have an asset mindset, guarding the data like they would guard money, and constantly making sure the systems they use for work don't double as home systems or become an inexpensive alternative to buying computers for a spouse or children.

2. Create and enforce policies. This goes for interoffice computing, travel computing, and home or telecommuter computing. This is a place that IT can really help determine guidelines and implement technology to help in preventing data leakage and unauthorized access. One company I know configures their laptops so that they cannot share files between home systems. There is some inconvenience here, but the trade off is worth it.

3. Use file name conventions that will be harder to search. For instance, filenames that have SSN, budget, salaries, or "passwords" in them should not be allowed. P2P users find these searching file names, not contents.

4. IT can also test P2P networks, using automated tools to look for information that might be associated with your

company. This is like looking for a needle in a haystack, but may be worth a try, particularly if you have distinctive file naming conventions. I have set up Google to constantly search for my name. Stelzl is pretty distinctive, and David Stelzl is almost completely distinctive.

5. Finally, there are services out there that will search for you, and it may be worth paying for if you're a large organization. Tiversa out of Pittsburg is one such company. This company provides P2P monitoring and risk assessment services for banks, credit card issuers, and insurers, as well as some government entities.

System Administrators Bend the Rules

We have just covered what I call the weakest link, the uninformed data user. But this topic is incomplete without a discussion on the IT organization. Data owners also need to know that data administration is being carried out in a restrictive manner.

I worked in an IT organization earlier in my career and clearly remember setting up systems to ease the burden of administration.

We had our servers linked together, allowing administrators to go from server to server without any sort of access control. Administrative IDs were called Admin and shared among all who had authorization, which included almost anyone in IT. That meant that all of us had unrestricted access without accountability, all using the same ID and password.

Many of our workstations had remote control software installed to ease administration. Similar software was set up across a large bank network to make remote administration easier.

I remember the day someone sent my manager a list of bank employee salaries with a written note that said, "How secure are these systems?" We never did find out who did this, but it was clear that our security was an afterthought. It should also be noted, we were not liable for these security weaknesses but it sure made us look bad.

As I said, this goes on today. In a recent phone call, an alarmed executive explained that someone had sent out incriminating email from his account. He wanted to know who did it. Since all of his administrators had rights and all used the same login credentials, there wasn't any way to tell, and of course everyone claimed to know nothing about it.

Where Compromises Occur

In summary, data is compromised when it is placed in the hands of unaware users and administrators, where short-cuts are taken to ease the job, and where the value of the asset is not communicated to those it is entrusted with.

Mobile data is easily stolen when stored on well marked laptops, mobile storage devices, or when travelers don't keep in mind the dollar value of the data, but instead only consider the device value.

Data is also easily stolen when unaware users have P2P and unsecure email applications, or have bought into schemes that use spam email or fraudulent websites to install remote control applications that provide unrestricted access to hackers over the Internet.

Creating the Restrictive Asset Mindset

The restrictive mindset values the data so much that the owner is unwilling to grant access without properly communicating its value. This mindset tests those entrusted on the level of responsibility each one will give to it as they use and administer the data. While I am not advocating a big brother approach or micro-management, I do see this like an accounting group that has strict guidelines, audits, and separation of duty. Some things to consider include:

Frequent user awareness programs used to maintain a cautious position toward data.

Policies written and enforced to control data.

Access managed by centralized tools to ensure that users have the right amount of access as their jobs change, new people are hired, projects come and go and the value of data changes.

Federal regulations and compliance.

Asset owners are aware of the state of their data – who is accessing what, and when. They are kept aware through regular reporting of unauthorized access and authorized users conducting unauthorized activities.

Detection and response are well developed, and response is tested and timed on a regular basis.

Steps are taken to guard against data leakage as well as unsecure use from remote locations.

The Role of the CSO

Once again, the role of the CSO is to make sure asset owners are aware of trends, relevant threats and the risks associated with seemingly innocuous data. Without proper education, asset owners will not realize what is important and what is not. The CSO is in a unique position to create awareness at the asset owner level so that data users and data administrators can be properly informed. The company can then formulate a plan following the coverage model presented earlier in the book.

Educating the Organization

Educating the organization is an ongoing process. In the area of restrictiveness, a couple of points are relevant:

- Data users will need to understand the risks of having too much authority.
- Supervision will be required and must be an acceptable part of doing business with sensitive data. Data users must be willing to have divided responsibilities, keeping one data user from having all of the information in their possession.
- People will need to get used to operating with thin clients – systems that don't contain all of the data and applications resident on the system.

By creating a more restrictive mindset, owners, users and administrators work within the parameters given to them for their job. Access is given on a need to know basis. IDs and passwords are managed carefully, following the course of one's job function, from initial hiring through promotions and position changes, and on to job termination or other job status change. With these ideas in mind, we now need to have a more thorough understanding of what digital assets are and how they behave. This will be an essential part of building the asset mindset.

Dave Stelzl

Chapter 8

Mindset #3: Digitally Aware

Digital Assets are unlike any other assets a company has. It might be argued that 90% of a company's intellectual property is in digital form and that 50% of it is likely in email at any given time. This is an asset perhaps worth more than just about any other asset, yet it's so intangible that no one gives it the attention it deserves. A misunderstanding here could cost you your business.

Every day this asset is placed in inter-office envelopes, transported insecurely on portable media, transmitted across the one media accessed by our world's most feared organizations.

Sources of Assets

Digital assets are hard to keep track of. You're not always aware when they are created inside your company. Many managers, government officials and ignorant thieves have been surprised to find out that there were digital assets or digital fingerprints being left along a path they hoped would not be discovered.

Consider the news in March 2008, when a Detroit city governor was caught in an affair with a co-worker. Text messages discovered on his city-paid cell phone told a story that destroyed his marriage and his career. Had he known these assets existed, surely he would have taken steps to secure or erase them. Another Mayor in New York City was discovered this same month spending tens of thousands of dollars on high end prostitutes in the Washington DC area. He was caught by accident through an undercover investigation targeting tax evasion, and he'd left a trail of phone records and unauthorized expenditures that were charged to the city of New York. His apology only went so far. Ultimately he was forced to resign – who knows where his marriage will end up.

Asset creators may include:
- Credit card transactions
- Order entry
- Design drawings (CAD/CAM)
- Patents
- Email and Voice Mail
- Memos
- Spread sheets and financials
- Accounting data and banking data
- Electronic medical records
- Instant messages
- Blogs
- Phone call recordings such as in a call center

Wherever company financials, orders, plans and designs, or customer interaction is recorded, there are digital assets. But there are more sources such as logs recorded on servers, routers, and other applications.

The Data Owner's Viewpoint

From the data owner's perspective, anything that your department does that represents intellectual capital or customer information is proprietary. You must entrust it to your employees, knowing full well that not everyone is reliable 100% of the time. There will be operational errors that will lead to data leakage, as well as purposeful attempts to use information in a wrong way. There may even be organized plans to place someone in your department as a legitimate hire with mal-intent. The security of your data has a lot to do with your understanding of how it works, who wants it, and how they will get it. Part of this is understanding the difference between digital and physical assets, and knowing how to secure digital assets.

The Data Users Viewpoint

I've said many times, the best technology in the world cannot defend against a good social engineer. Nor can it help the data user once they have taken this data outside the boundaries set by the security program you have in place. In general, this group believes that IT has the security under control and that it is their duty to make sure data goes uncompromised regardless of where it is and who is using it.

Exposure happens when data is placed on insecure media, business systems are used for unauthorized tasks such as indiscriminant surfing of the web, and data users are fooled into giving up permission or downloading remote control applications that will be used by thieves. These users must learn an asset mindset and follow security measures, meaning they do not give out information unless certain criteria are met.

The System Administrator's Viewpoint

The administrator of any data is generally in a no-win situation. On one hand, companies hand security responsibilities to those who have not been trained well on security. In a recent event I had one IT attendee from a large well-known institution claim that none of his servers were accessible from the Internet. After further discussion, I asked, "Are you connected to the Internet?" He agreed the servers were. Then he noted that his firewall prevented all access, believing the most common misconception that having a firewall prevented all unauthorized access. This type of thinking is more common than you might think.

The Risk of Not Knowing

An interesting article appeared in *USA Today* on April 1, 2008 talking about the counter intelligence programs used in the US to provide daily briefings to the president. Each morning the president of the United States sits through a briefing to understand what threats the country is up against, what other governments are up to, who is building nuclear weapons, etc. This used to be accomplished by covert operations, sending people into unfriendly countries to spy, record and even steal confidential information to piece this together for government officials . Not anymore. The public Internet has replaced these activities as the primary source of intelligence. Something referred to Open-Source Intelligence or OSINT. This simply refers to a process of combing the Internet through automated and manual systems to uncover documents that were either purposely or accidentally placed in public areas on the Internet.

According to the article, intelligence workers have uncovered secret training manuals used by terrorist groups, plans and operations that are targeting and threatening the country, and the state of military activities. By searching on P2P networks, looking through documents written in other languages, and automating the process, almost anything can be found. If this highly sensitive information is out there, what else might be? Certainly your data is not more sensitive than theirs.

Of course there is the non-open-source side of this as well. Reports I have read in *USA Today* indicate that China employs at least 40,000 government sponsored hackers. In fact, over 120 countries currently have cyber divisions in process to watch what other governments are up to. So between OSINT and government cyber espionage, the secrets are getting out.

Your Business

If all of this exists on the government side, you can be sure corporate data is out there too. Design documents, strategic plans, financial data, and everything one needs to compete against your company is online somewhere. How long will it take the competition to put together an intelligence team to start researching this? Perhaps they already have one.

Nuclear secrets are one thing, but what about the data used every day by data users in your company? We refer to this as data leakage; intentional as well as unintentional leaking of data out of the corporation.

There may be employees that are taking data to competitors, as well as employees saving data they may want in the event of a future job change. We've discussed all the reason and ways data is taken home with workers, which frequently requires putting data in unsecure locations such as gmail accounts or portable media devices that may be lost or forgotten. How often does someone put data on a thumb drive and then forget about it once the project is complete? It's just a copy, and so it may be tossed in a drawer or thrown in a computer bag, and later discarded unintentionally.

Emailing confidential information without some sort of encryption (something missing in most corporate computing practices), is always a no-no. Yet, in an effort to get the job done, workers regularly send account numbers, credit card numbers and company confidential data through unsecure email applications for approvals, comments, collaboration, and any number of things in the name of saving time.

The assumption is that IT has it covered. When data users access applications, whether in the office, at home, or on the road, the assumption is that security is a technical issue and that IT has put controls in place to make sure things are safe. Data owners need to educate data users that security is a people problem, not simply a practice of using firewalls.

Adding to the problem, data users over time become numb to the sensitivity of most applications they access. Of course there are top secret jobs out there that come with constant reminders, but much of the data is seen as just part of the job. All of this leads to lax data security practices, demands for increased access rights, and less accountability between workers and managers.

Be sure, if government secrets are out there, your company data is too. Getting it back is not going to be easy. In fact, it's impossible. All you can do at this point is focus on preventing further data leakage.

Personal Data

And of course this same problem affects personal data. While this book is not meant to address personal data protection, it deserves mentioning that the same problems exists at home, and maybe to a greater degree. Add home security to the problem of people taking work home with company data, and this problem becomes a big one.

Just think, every URL and webpage you've ever accessed, and many of the emails you've read were tied to digital assets somewhere on someone's computer. Every transaction is tied to a credit card, even if the vendor claimed "discreet billing," and is recorded so it could be revealed at some point either for marketing, subpoena, or as a result of someone hacking into another company's database.

Understanding the Digital Asset

The digital asset is unlike any other. You can't look at a hard drive or a wire and see it, or look in the sky and see assets flying from one computer to another, yet they are there and can be captured.

Most of us are thinking our assets are safe in the data center. Yet the data is not there.

Yes, there is a copy of the data in the data center, but the data in use is also in motion. It's traversing Ethernet networks, satellite, microwave, wireless networks, and the Internet; mostly in insecure ways such as email. Remember, when digital assets are stolen, you still have them – you'll never miss them, and so you'll never know when someone has taken them. Perhaps most importantly, when you decide to erase them, they are not really gone.

Creating the Digitally Aware Asset Mindset

The two groups of people most likely to misunderstand the nature of this asset are the data owners and data users. As a result, IT may be asked to secure data, more through assumption than actual request. The administrator is set up for failure. Some steps that can be taken to create this mindset include:

- Creating data policies that govern data through the entire life-cycle.
- Insisting that data be classified by data owners and educated data creators – this will help communicate the importance and sensitivity to those accessing and using data.
- Deploying technologies that prevent data leakage through email, data duplication to mobile devices based on policy, and encryption standards on mobile computing devices as well as email applications.
- Consistent, user focused, user awareness training programs that demonstrate the creation, classification, and security requirements associated with the data created and used by each department.

The digitally aware person recognizes that data is being created through every application. It's not just an order for a product or request for hotel or car rental. It's data being handed to a provider to get a service, or data being recorded in a transaction or phone call. Then that data, now an asset, is someone's responsibility. It must be protected, safeguarded and treated like personal money if it is to be kept safe. With this in mind, let's realize that people are after this asset and so we must be alert. The alert mindset is next.

Chapter 9

Mindset #4: Alert vs. Lockdown

Security should be built on the assumption that hackers will get in. Security strategies generally assumes they won't. Protective barriers around buildings are always backed by detection, but much of today's computer security has no real detection in place. Castles have high walls and, if built by wise architects, a view that allows the defending army to see what's coming. IT rarely has this advantage.

Data centers are not castles, and no matter how far into the mountains we build them, they are always accessible and advertised universally online. The data they house is needed by corporate users working from regional offices, home offices and public areas including airports and hotels, both locations notorious for data thieves. Here the "Alert Mindset" is set against the traditional "Keep Out" mindset. We need to understand that data is required by businesses universally not only to the company's internal users, but also to a myriad of external users including partners, customers, and what may be referred to as "co-opertition."

Data is no longer contained within the data center, being accessed by green screen computers, but is moving more and more to a mobile and wireless computing model. Companies have no choice but to assume the wrong people will gain access to corporate systems.

The Traditional Mindset

I've discussed how the traditional view on security is to treat it as a technical problem. Data owners assume that IT will protect the data as fast as their employees can create it, IT knows the value of the data or that IT automatically secures all data. There are two incorrect traditional mindsets emerging here by data owners and users and then by those managing the IT side.

Data owners and users may incorrectly think:
- **The Traditional Mindset Means: Keep out**

When in fact:
- **Data requires universal access**
- **Detection requires constant monitoring**
- **Logs can be changed, tracks covered**

Balance Security – No silos

The assumption was made long ago that we would be able to keep out the attacker with the right technology such as encryption and firewalls. Now most IT people would not deny that attackers can get in, but there are still many companies that believe their systems are secure. Most underestimate the technology and social engineering techniques used by intruders. Companies are living in a make-believe, "safe" world.

But even those who understand that attackers can get in underestimate the risks associated with data theft and loss. I hear things like, "Who would want our data? After all, we aren't a large bank." This thinking is a problem. Every company is in danger if it has meaningful data, financial data, or information relevant to competition, potential lawsuits of unhappy customers or anything someone can profit from. Recent articles on the subject of targets indicate that small and mid-market companies are becoming a larger target for criminals due to the lack of security they employ. In other words, criminals can easily break through small business security and their data is just as valuable.

Detection – The First Step to Defending

Better detection, is the first step to improving overall protection. While the first column in our security architecture, protection, is proactive and preventative, keeping everyone out is the hardest and most expensive aspect of the security architecture to implement, but it is the protection strategy that sets up the line or policy that will be detected when compromised. Assume it will be compromised. The line is always crossed at some point, and if there is no detection, your data is at risk. The good news is that a sound detection program can make up for having less protection in place.

The Alert mindset assumes that the breech is coming or is in process somewhere in the company. If you hear someone breaking into your home during the night, you know you need to be ready to respond. It may never actually happen in the physical world, and I am hoping it doesn't happen to you or me. On the physical side most of us have less risk of this break-in simply because house break-ins are not automated. If someone could figure out a way to hit all of the houses on your street without having to visit each one, they would. But it's simply too time consuming and the chances of getting caught, too high. On the Internet, this is not so.

The alert mindset understands that attacks will be stealth and automated to some point. It may start with social engineering such as a phone call to an administrative office worker or security person, but at some point technology will be used to access the data. Smaller companies are getting hit harder as more automation comes into play. These attacks are not like someone crashing through your back doors in mid-day with guns, but rather more like a night time, covert military operation. They get in without being seen, set up equipment that will allow for continuous surveillance, and then get out quietly.

Cyber attacks in many ways parallel a stealth physical attack. The research is done up front, most of which will be perfectly legal to do, like sitting in front of a house, watching from a car window. The stalker observers the going and coming of homeowners, looking for patterns that represent holes in security. They notice no one is home between certain hours, or one of the parents trend to travel on certain days. The parents leave a key under the back door mat that gets used when children come home from school. Perhaps they always enter through the garage, signaling to the observer that this is the door that does not sound the alarm immediately when entering.

The intruder will want to know who the people are, what kinds of things they own, and where the key assets may be located. The same will be true for a company break-in or cyber attack. The intruder will comb your site for information on physical locations, business focus, data center locations, and whatever Internet related information they can come up with. Again, most of this is legal and undetectable.

Next is probing the systems. The true professional will be on the phone acting as a potential client, investor, IT worker, office worker, or whatever they can come up with to gather information inside. They start by learning the language, understanding the protocols, and figuring out where security lines are drawn. Some of these techniques may border on illegal, and will certainly be unethical, but will not be easily traceable if they know what they are doing.

In the process, your employees will be talked into giving out passwords, downloading malicious software, and possibly giving out or emailing sensitive documents. In more automated scenarios used in the small and medium size business world, you'll find that legitimate websites are being compromised using malware that infects your system. You may wonder how they get away with this.

Hackers put malware on sites you use just long enough to compromise a few thousand computers, and then the overseers of that site discover and remove it. However, the damage is already done. You're infected and the intruder is in.

All of this takes time but it is often less detectable than physically breaking into a building. Even the trained eye will not spot every technology breech.

The only hope is having a sound detection process in place. Detection depends on the protection strategy being set up properly. This then creates the tripwire to sound the alarm. If your door is wide open, setting your alarm won't actually work.

The Alert Mindset Starts with Educating People

When security is regarded as a technical problem, IT is over worked and the technology is generally insufficient. Creating the alert mindset starts with the people who create and use data, not with technology. The Alert Mindset requires a strong detection program which is built alongside the protection program, putting into action ways to discover misuse or policy breech before its too late.

A great detection program starts with a continuous evaluation program to uncover (or detect) weaknesses in the security strategy. We will deal more with this in the chapter on interrogation and assessment, but here we'll focus on detecting attacks or instances that are actually happening or predictable.

There are countless scams out there. Recently I received a call from a call center announcing that I had won a free trip to a Florida resort. I don't know about you, but at the time that sounded pretty good. This had nothing to do with the computer, so perhaps it was real. The initial call promised a free stay at a fancy resort if I would agree to a 90 minute tour of the facilities. The picture became a little clearer at this point. I hadn't actually won anything;

I had qualified as a prospect based on my income bracket. This was a free lunch to sell me something. But how do you know something like this is for real, or just a scam to collect personal data. You don't.

Well trained people fall for these sales pitches every day, and many times fall more than once. The social engineering tactics are built using the same tactics, to gain the trust of people who have needs, are somewhat self confident, and don't want to hurt other's feelings. They don't want to appear prudish by asking to see ID before they let someone piggyback through the keycard entry door. Con artists study the weaknesses of people before planning their attacks and then prey on them. The success rate is high, just like a strong marketing plan.

The alert mindset involves training knowledge workers to see a violation of policy, to know what to do about it, and to be willing to take action. A culture must be created that allows workers to question managers if they don't see a badge, or are asked to give information out that would violate a policy. There must be a process for gaining approval on weekends or after hours, before the policy is broken, and in time to respond to a real need. After all, some of these requests are legitimate. Setting up a detection system alerts your team to break-ins and misuse, especially those on the inside. Even creating the fear that someone will get caught decreases the potential of unethical employees making mistakes.

Technology Automates Detection

Once your people understand the security issues and policies are in place, a detection strategy is beginning to take shape. This is where the complexity comes in. Some detection will have to be manual, such as spotting an authorized user doing something that violates policy. If someone brings food into the computer room, this is likely a breach of policy and someone will have to see this to stop it.

But there are many technologies available providing different levels of detection, including:

- Failed login attempts signaling that someone is attempting to find the right password.
- Users accessing inappropriate sites (As defined by your organization). Many of these sites will contain malware waiting to be installed on your site.
- Computers accessing P2P networks while also connected to the corporate network.
- Malicious code making outbound calls from a workstation.

While there are far too many items to list here, my point is there are tools that can detect if a computer is being used in a way that will expose the company to danger. Doing this manually never works. Don't believe someone is looking at the logs because log data is cryptic and overwhelming. The process of event gathering and analysis must be automated.

The Alert Mindset Involves a Timed Response

A few years ago I was working with an online company in New York that used web applications connected to a backend application. We discovered some major holes in their security but found they had an intrusion detection system in place, actually being monitored around the clock by a well known third party organization. Still, hackers gained access to their internal network, changing the passwords on every router, switch and server.

I got the call at 11:00 AM the next morning – they had been hacked. I learned the breach was detected at 3:00 AM, more than six hours earlier. The VP's first question, "Should we disconnect from the Internet?" really alarmed me. Why were they asking this question, when it was clear that they could not access their systems and someone else could through the Internet? They had some level of detection, but clearly no response.

Response Must be Real Time

"Real Time" is a computer term that can mean a lot of things. It doesn't mean "instant," but rather the ability to affect a situation within a predetermined time frame, which is generally very short in computer speak. When we say, "The response must be real time," we simply mean that the detection happens fast enough to react in such a way that the data remains safe. We beat the perpetrator to the punch. In the Internet, this often has to be so fast that it seems instant.

When banks are robbed, the robber first has to determine if the bank's response plan works. If it looks too good, they will move on to a new bank. The robber could break in at night, but they know most response plans will work at night. It's better to break in during daylight hours. It sounds backwards, but it's not.

In the daytime, the safe is open, and of course, the doors are open too. The robber enters the bank, takes out the cameras and moves people away from alarm buttons. If they know the safe is open, it'll take seconds to collect the money. They also know that the police are going to take several minutes or longer to respond once they get the call, which in most cases is true. This provides plenty of time.

At night the scene is much different. The door is locked and the alarm is set. Once the door is broken and the alarm triggered, the response plan timer begins. They have a fixed number of minutes to get in, break open the safe, take the money and get out. The problem is, the safe manufacturer has already thought this through. It's not that the safe can't be cracked, it can. But the manufacturer has already figured out how long this will take and has rated the safe to indicate this timing to the buyer. So depending on the location of the bank and the value of assets planned for this location, the bank can plan their response.

Let's say it will take 30 minutes to crack the safe with a torch. If the bank has worked this out properly, the police will get there in far less time on average. Assuming they have a response plan that works, the money is safe.

The Response Must be Effective

One night I was trying to sleep in my tent on a backpacking trip, thinking about safety after hearing about a gruesome crime committed against two women backpacking in the Shenandoah Mountains. Some of my children were with me on this trip, so every animal noise, twig cracking and even the sound of the wind somehow sounded like an intruder. Needless to say, I didn't get much sleep that night.

At some point in the night it occurred to me, as I lie as still as possible, that my protective barrier was rip-stop nylon. My detection was pretty good because I was wide awake, listening to every noise. However, my response plan was almost non-existent. What could I do? I wouldn't be able to run since I had the kids. I am not really equipped to put up a good fight against a couple of thugs – I missed out on Karate lessons as a kid. I had my Swiss army knife, but so what? Maybe I could whittle a small spear but I didn't have a stick in my tent.

My next purchase following that trip was a small firearm, although luckily I have never had to use it. I also bought a can of bear spray in case the intruder is bigger than expected and covered with brown fur.

The bottom line is: your response has to be effective. When data intruders get in, they don't make a lot of noise. Also, a smart intruder may create numerous false positives so we'll be accustomed to hearing the noises. We may be tricked into turning the alarm off, and then the thief strikes for real.

Alertness Requires a Balanced PDR Strategy

Alertness is balanced by PDR – building all three columns. As we said, most IT security is mostly P – Protection. There may be pieces of the D –Detection, and R – Response columns, but the model is out of balance. We expect Protection to work for a period of time or until a professional arrives. The true point of protection is to trigger Detection, and then Response must be there in real-time.

The model is balanced when we start with protection, detection and response. We add some more protection, then more detection and response, building the model across like stacking bricks next to each other. The model invests in protection technology like firewalls and passwords to keep out the honest people, as well as the automated garbage like spam and other low level unauthorized traffic.

In parallel, the company is investing in, or contracting out, a much more sophisticated detection scheme. Security companies can provide 24/7 monitoring. Larger companies have their own physical security operations center, which you might carry over to IT, building the Information Technology equivalent.

Creating the Alert Mindset

As in every mindset, the Alert mindset must exist across the three types of people that touch data: data owners, data users and data custodians. Remember that security is never just a technology problem. Here are some of the considerations that should be considered as you build this mindset into your organization:

- Data owners must have a way to hold data users accountable for the data they touch. This is no different than balancing a cash register at the end of the day. Somewhere along the line, people got the idea that email and instant messaging are private tools to be used in private. In business, this is not true. Policy should tell everyone that company systems are company property, and are auditable by company management. Encourage people to establish their own personal email accounts for home use through a secure email provider. I discourage the use of free email services.

- This same concept must go up the management chain. Executives have at times used work computers for their own personal use. There needs to be a cultural shift so that managers know their systems will be monitored by someone with authority and therefore won't use these systems for anything they would not want authorized managers to see. This type of disclosure may have saved the mentioned governors some embarrassment.

- Divide responsibilities so that it takes more than one person to access certain types of information. This may create some extra work, but it's worth it. This is the case in accounting, and we live with it because it is money. Computer systems have this same type of value in many cases. They either have the financial data or the intellectual capital that keeps the company in business. This is worth protecting.

Dave Stelzl

- Train data users how to spot violations of policies and find ways to encourage them to report breaches. This may be the biggest hurdle, but it's necessary. Create a way for people to report problems anonymously.

- Provide a clear set of steps to take when asked for certain information. For instance, if an executive calls an employee at home on a weekend, with an emergency, there needs to be a process in place to allow that to happen. This is similar to a lock box or escrow account. The employee might notify IT of the need, and IT might have a way to provide the executive with what they need. This works well with password resets.

- Begin using technology to automate as many of the detection processes as possible.

Company data will be much safer when the Alert Mindset is present across all who create, use or manage data.

Chapter 10

Mindset #5 Ready to Respond

At about eleven o'clock one evening I was lying in bed in a New York city hotel room when my cell phone range. My caller ID told me that it was my father calling, who would normally be fast asleep by now. My imagination began running wild.

"Your alarm company just called and your alarm is going off, but they cannot reach anyone at the house!" Where was my family, and why were they not answering the phone? I had spoken to my wife around 9:00 PM that same evening and the kids were all either in bed or headed that way. I began to panic.

My father offered to drive over to my house and see what was going on, but I wanted to try cell phones and my home office line first. After two unsuccessful attempts, I was able to reach one of my daughters on my home office line. They were all upstairs, and sure enough, the alarm was ringing. I could hear it in the background. The display indicated a front window break and my wife was on the phone with our local police department. The kids thought they had heard someone downstairs, but the house was now silent. One child reported seeing a flash of light in the front yard, but they weren't sure from where.

My wife informed the police that she was armed and that they should let her know when they arrived. They reported back that they were 20 minutes away! But they'd be there as quickly as possible. Somehow 20 minutes didn't sound like a reasonable response time for this type of incident.

As part of their protocol, they asked to her to put the gun away, but she let them know that this was not an option given the 20 minute wait. Something was wrong with this whole response plan. What happens when an alarm works, but the timing of the response plan is out of line with the requirements?

It turned out our alarm was a false positive. A falling wash basket had set off the alarm so there actually wasn't an emergency at all. However it took 20 minutes to figure this out. If this had been an actual break-in and the perpetrator hadn't run from the alarm, serious damage might have occurred. My family could have been hurt, or my wife might have felt the need to defend the castle, resulting in all kinds of legal issues as to whether or not such force was actually required.

When response plans don't respond quickly enough, the security plan fails badly. As we move from the Alert mindset to the "Ready-to-Respond" mindset, we will talk about what makes a great protection/detection plan verses a worthless one. This vital step shows you how to have the mindset of being ready to respond with an effective response plan.

Poorly Executed Response

Here's another failed response example that is close to home for me. As a teenager, I went through every Red Cross swimming class available. Toward my college age years, I held several certifications including my Water Safety Instructor Card (WSI) which allowed me to train and certify other lifeguards. I taught classes at various camps, issuing cards to young aspiring lifeguards, and I also served as a lifeguard at several camp pools and on the waterfront of a New York based wilderness camp in the Adirondacks. One day the moment of truth came; the real test of practiced response.

Up until that day, I had never had the opportunity to pull someone out of the water. For some reason, people just didn't get into trouble when I was on duty, and I didn't guard high risk environments. But one day I was asked to take a group down to the south shore of Long Island, a considerably rough ocean beach with strong riptides and cold water. We were early that day so there were only a few people around while my group was about 20 in size, and mostly good swimmers. My job was to stand on the beach and watch, keep people within a restricted area and to save anyone in the unlikely event that someone got in real trouble.

The unlikely occurred and a young lady got caught in a riptide and was drifting out away from land. While not too dramatic, she was in fact in trouble. She was a good swimmer but could not make it back to where she could touch ground. As I contemplated what to do, she drew further and further away. By the time I realized that she actually needed help, she was really far out there. I kept hoping that she'd start making some progress back to shore, but she didn't. I was frozen in disbelief. Was I going to just let this happen?

The waves were big and for the first time, lesson number one in lifeguarding became real. I needed some sort of flotation device to safely venture out into the open sea and get her. You never risk your own life by going in with just yourself, especially in the ocean. Drowning victims will do anything to stay above water, including pull their lifesaver under. The principle was theoretical but I knew the truth.

An incredible fear seized me because I felt I was not equipped to respond to this emergency! I watched as she continued to head out from the land, wondering what to do. I had no idea what to do, I couldn't even yell for help. There was no one there who could help me.

Suddenly an ocean trained lifeguard, employed by the beach, came out of nowhere, running past me with his trusty torpedo PDF (Personal flotation device) and began to charge through the waves to reach my victim. I have no idea where he came from or how long he had been on the beach, but his response was swift and effective, and I was extremely thankful. It was obvious that he had the training and experience, and therefore was equipped to carry out an effective plan.

He could have said something to me, but he didn't. I was clearly at fault and completely unprepared to do my job. I left humbled by this scene and promised myself to never again take on the job of responding without proper training and equipment, and thanking God that there was a backup.

The lesson I learned applies to technology as well. Security fails when the response plan is theoretical, untested, and the responder is ill-equipped. Security fails when the timing is not calculated beforehand to ensure a timely rescue. Detection must be flawless and response must be well prepared and alert, ready to respond before assets are compromised.

Lessons Learned

Events that "never happen" are hard to protect against. It takes practice and the proper equipment to respond effectively. I continued lifeguarding in non-ocean environments, and later in my guarding career had the opportunity to successfully rescue several campers as I watched over the camp waterfront. Each time I was equipped with my PDF, either throwing a ring or jumping in with a torpedo. I had learned my lesson, and was grateful no lives were lost in the process. I am also happy to report that at home, we have never experienced an actual break-in or have ever had to act with deadly force, although we are prepared.

Whether it's a break-in, a waterfront emergency or many other types of emergencies, response takes practice. People who respond well have often learned from past mistakes. When someone responds with excellence to an emergency, they have been well trained and have likely practiced frequently. Response has to become a natural reaction or automated computer response or it just won't work, at least not in a predictable way.

Responding to Cybercrime

Firewalls can always be beat, just as safes are always rated to allow the owner to prepare an adequate response plan. Banks actually time the response when they put the safe in. They know how far away the police station is and can predict how long it will take help to arrive given a break-in.

Imagine if firewall manufacturers took this approach and labeled their products accordingly. How long would you have? Would it be hours, minutes, seconds? Or would the thief simply bypass the firewall, using social engineering tactics and insider connections to gain access to what they want?

"This new firewall is supposed to take at least 20 seconds to break through!"

If using a fire wall is the major part of the security plan, the security strategy would likely pivot around keeping people out. But security that depends on keeping people out also depends on keeping people in, and when this happens, like in our house analogy, the system becomes unusable. People operate in a mobile world today and keeping data inside the glass house is no longer an option. And now with the advent of cloud-computing, where companies depend more on hosted software as a service, third-party hosted data-centers, and even storage on demand hosted by an outside company, the secure data center concept becomes outdated and inadequate for future applications.

In the end, it is not going to be possible to secure anything through protection strategies so the challenge becomes making data and applications accessible almost universally, while still maintaining some level of security. This will have to depend on detection, and with this, there will have to be a well timed response plan. When our mindset doesn't consider mobile data access, the mindset is wrong.

Data continues to grow in complexity as we merge voice, video and data into large scale data centers that will be accessed by people globally. The use of social networking sites, instant messaging, voice using the IP network, and mobility using personally owned systems such as PDAs is here to stay and will only grow. If IT departments try to restrict this, they will lose the battle. Revenue generation always wins over restrictive security policies. It's not enough to just say, "you'll be held responsible if you lose the data," because in the end it's the company, shareholders and executives that will be affected the most.

The Role of Data Users

Traditionally it is IT Security's job to make sure there is a response plan in place, but this poses some serious problems. The point of greatest vulnerability is at the end-user level, and it is also true that the early detection process is most effective at the departmental level. Co-workers generally know when people are sending information over unsecure networks. It becomes an acceptable practice, and perhaps no one really knows the difference. The beginning of detection and response is in equipping and training the end-users at a departmental level.

End-users need to know:
- What data is sensitive.
- Who would want such data.
- What would be the impact of losing this data.
- What policies govern sensitive data.
- What should a co-worker do if they witness policy violations.
- And are they willing to take such action?

In a recent lunch meeting with corporate IT executives in New York City, one attendee asked me how to get the attention of senior executives in his company. He said, "They don't want any restrictions, yet the data must be secure." Well, to start, people must be educated about attack methods and where spyware is getting in. Showing execs how this can be used to compromise data goes a long way. Demonstrations oriented to non-technical users also go a long way. Another solution is through penetration testing, where security experts discover data (often referred to as trophies) to prove how easy it is to gain access to sensitive data. These trophies illustrate how big the problem really is. Executives are frequently surprised when a penetration attack is successful, yet I know of very few that weren't.

Companies need to provide their employees with simple-to-use tools that encrypt data when it's taken home. Employees need to be able to compute securely from home. Having people email data to a home PC that is shared by high-schoolers is not going to be a safe place for corporate data, but again, this must be proven by demonstration. Strong response plans start with regular training and demonstrations at the departmental level.

In addition, I recommend having a contact inside any major department that understands the security response plan in the event of an attack. This person can help coordinate response plans in the face of large scale attacks, operator errors or environmental events such as the recent hurricane hitting the gulf regions in Texas. This helps by expanding the size of the response team without adding headcount to IT. It also puts IT in touch with the impacts and affects of downed systems and loss of data at the departmental level.

The Role of Data Owners

While data users represent the greatest point of weakness in the IT security strategy, data owners represent some of the greatest insight into what is critical and what is needed to carry on a competitive business plan. Without a strong business plan, the company cannot compete in today's global economy. So if the plan developed by IT to secure data does not include collaboration with data owners, chances are it won't meet the company's departmental business needs. This will result in greater resistance from the department and departmental leadership, and companies might actually create work-a-rounds without IT's knowledge; such as putting in their own wireless networks and other security-bypassing schemes. Of course when they do this, they open the company up to all kinds of threats.

Senior departmental management can help IT understand what the response time should be. They can provide contacts within departments to train on response plans, and help support whatever steps are required to build an adequate response program that is in line with departmental functional requirements.

The Role of IT

IT security and IT in general, manage the technology infrastructure and applications that may be attacked by both insiders and outsiders. When security fails, it may be the result of an attack or it may be operator or system error. All three of these are security problems in that they affect data privacy, integrity or data availability, or perhaps all three in some combination.

When operator error or system failures occur, one type of response is needed. When it's a crime, an entirely different scenario takes place. First, let's consider operator error or system failure. This is by far the more likely scenario when dealing with down time situations or loss of system access. Most attacks today are attempts to steal information and are therefore not focused on system disruption, although there are exceptions. IT's responsibility is to plan for business continuity by understanding the business impact of system disruption through assessments, making recommendations that increase system continuity, and carrying out an approved course of action. If a disruptive event causes significant loss of information, disaster recovery plans must be put in place for responding to an emergency, providing backup operations, and managing the recovery process. These events are not really the focus of this book, but should be carefully studied to develop proper business continuity and disaster recovery planning procedures for the organization.

But when there's an attack, there are major decisions that must be made and tension develops between IT and data owners/users. Do we get the system back up and running, or do we work through a forensics investigation to determine what happened and perhaps who was involved? Note that the two are mutually exclusive. When the goal is to get the system back up and running, it destroys the evidence. When the team investigates and preserves any evidence, the system remains unusable. It's a trade off.

I once worked with a technology company to help them put security strategies in place for one of their clients, a local hospital. We weren't far into it when we received a call from the CIO explaining that someone had hacked into the system and erased the backup system. Since no applications were affected, the hospital chose to work on getting the system back into production which would take a few days, based on the resource availability.

The next night another attack occurred, taking out the billing system. Without a backup in place, and the billing system corrupted, the hospital was in seriously bad shape. An investigation showed that an IT administrator had been terminated a few days before and wasn't on good terms with the hospital. We suspected this person to be the perpetrator.

The hospital could not operate without their billing system, and so they again chose restoration over investigation. The problem is that the evidence and chain of custody are broken when the system is restored. It's like walking into a crime scene and touching everything, moving things around, and perhaps even dusting and painting. Anything that could have led to prosecution is no longer admissible in court. As a result, the suspect goes free. This is a common issue among cybercrimes today.

Computer crime has many faces, and new ones are constantly evolving.

Attacks can:
- take out systems such as Denial of Service,
- overload web facing servers to the point of making them unusable,
- eavesdrop on or capture real-time communications during the exchange of data or network voice applications,
- lead to fraudulent selling,
- include software piracy,
- use malicious code to either destroy or spy on someone,
- use Trojan software programs that steal surreptitiously, as in the TJ Max case.
- use acts of espionage or pretexting (pretending to be someone you are not through email of a chat program), embezzlement, terrorism, and the list goes on.

IT must be prepared to take a leadership role in responding to these types of acts – particularly those that pose the greatest threat to the organization, called the relevant threats.

IT should first of all be educating the organization how to conduct a response, the importance of being prepared to investigate and to carry out a proper investigation when something like this happens.

IT should either have the capability internally to do this, or have a relationship with a company that is trained to respond.

This book is not about forensics. There are entire books on this subject explaining the many detailed steps that must take place during a recovery process in order to preserve evidence and maintain the chain of evidence. Understanding the laws that apply to computer crimes, how to determine if a crime has occurred, and how to preserve the evidence are all part of the IT security role.

Computer forensics involve the collecting of information surrounding the attack in such as way that it will be admissible in a court of law. Because all of this is done electronically, there are a number of gray areas and complexities in collecting and preserving this evidence. Investigations are often under strict time frames so that systems aren't tied up for prolonged periods of time.

Once systems are updated and back into production, the evidence is no longer admissible. Therefore the gathering, control, and preservation of evidence are extremely important. It's easy to tamper with digital evidence, so control of it is essential to the process. Investigators have to show that they obtained the evidence at the right crime scene, that it was gathered right after the crime was committed, who found it, when, who secured it and how it has been maintained.

With all of this in mind, proper response requires planning ahead. The team must prepare to handle the process, know who will be involved, and must know what steps to take to preserve evidence without putting the company out of business due to a long investigation period.

Define Your Response

At the Federal level, there is a group call CERT (Computer Emergency Response Team), but at the local level there should also be a CIRT (Spelled differently to avoid confusion). CIRT will stand for Computer Incident Response Team. It's a team that you put together, train, and provide time for to rehearse the protocol to be used in the event of an incident.

A well organized CIRT Team can provide leadership to each department involved, help in the case of investigation, and know how to preserve any require evidence if the event involves a criminal act.

There are other types of response that should be understood and considered, especially at the asset owner level. It's important to plan ahead and know where each response is best applied.

Mitigation is perhaps the most cost effective and most important response. It simply means heading off the crime before it happens. Larger companies generally assess security on some periodic basis or when compliance demands it. Smaller companies, on the other hand, tend to bypass the assessment, thinking it's unnecessary and costly, or because they lack the resources. In either case, assessments are critical and should assess risk levels and not just vulnerabilities.

The purpose of this response is fixing any areas of the system that lack security. These areas may be education, using protocols dealing with certain types of assets, technology choices or other policy changes that defend against both internal and external attacks. The more attention we can give this situation up front, the less reactive your response will need to be later on. The bottom line is, losses will be reduced.

Reaction-Response is simply a reaction to an attack. I often find policies to have a complete lack of response or enforcement. What happens when someone breaks a policy? Is there a stated consequence? If not, the policy is reduced into just a recommendation with nothing to back it up.

When malicious code enters the system, there is often an automated response. Software stops and cleans the virus from the system, assuming there was a signature or some way to detect the presence of malicious code. So here we see two types of response: human intervention to stop a violation of policy (which could be a part of an attack) and an automated response through antivirus software.

Both are valid responses, although automated responses may be quicker and are able to remove or stop things easier than a person. The downside, as already stated, is that programs don't have the mental capability to make decisions in the case of unexpected behavior. So both response types are needed.

Recovery Response occurs after something has been compromised, and damage must be repaired.

In cases of a hurricane, like one that recently hit the gulf coast of Texas, people and companies have to leave the affected cities. If they had a well constructed disaster recovery plan, perhaps they were able to open up operations in remote locations overnight. In our case, we were without gas for weeks. In the case of the hospital, technicians were dispatched to recover data that had been erased. Hopefully, there were backups with somewhat recent data available. The cost of these types of responses is high and should be minimized.

Forensics is also a type of reactive response that needs to be well thought out ahead of time. If not, the likelihood of gathering the right data in the right way, so that it will be admissible in court, is low. *USA Today* recently cited a study conducted back in 2005, stating that 75% of all attacks include an insider, and insiders are able to hide the evidence or make it no longer useful to a court system or investigation.

A final response may be thought of as a **counter attack**, which is hard to plan out beforehand. It makes most sense in the context of cyberwarfare, where it can be proven that another government has launched attacks in the same way military organizations might launch a missile. On the corporate side, it would generally be considered illegal in the United States to launch this type of attack against a competitor or individual. Forensics investigation and proper prosecution would be the acceptable approach.

Responses That Don't Work

All of the responses above can work, on the other hand, they can all be performed badly. Two problems arise when companies are not prepared to respond or are not equipped to respond. A third problem is responding to the wrong problem or having too many problems to respond to.

Hackers simply create an issue that requires a response, tying up a companies response resources, and then making another attack against that same company in another area. It's a diversion similar to a football play. This can be an effective strategy against large financial institutions, but if you work in a small or midsize firm, the likelihood is low and should be not be a major focus.

Another angle is to trigger alarms over and over to upset the response system until someone shuts it off, which then creates an open door for the attacker. This angle happens more often than the first method since it is easy to do and quite effective.

The solution here is to apply the concepts of defense in depth using automation. When one response fails, another is waiting.

Finally, response that is never tested often does not work. Having a protocol is good, but testing it is much better. The response process should be easy to carry out. A simple, well executed, plan works better than sophisticated plans that are poorly executed. Sports teams that can execute a few plans very well beat the competition when playing against a team that focuses on complex strategies that they are unable to pull off.

A simple escalation plan is a great start. It's not uncommon for an administrator to hesitate when experiencing an issue. Calling senior management over a weekend, when you're not sure if you should, seems too risky. Instead, they take matters into their own hands and hope to resolve the issues without interrupting someone's family time. This can lead to greater unexpected interruptions or may encourage them to make a decision they're not authorized to make. This is another incorrect response.

Consider a night time security person who doesn't have a protocol to use when faced with an unexpected, urgent request. They may think some senior exec has made the request. Not knowing what else to do, they may give out information or allow access to a con artist working out a clever scheme. When this happens, security fails.

Responses That Work Well

These are simple and well rehearsed. The entire team is informed, including asset owners, asset users, and those responsible for technical systems management. This education will assist them in making heat-of-the-moment decisions. Plans are great until the war hits, and then all of the sudden everything is contingent on what happens next. On the spot decisions need to be made. People should have a clear understanding of what the main objectives are for this system, and what data is critical. This generally means involving an asset owner if the process is not already thought out and defined.

Security events that require human intervention are rare, so team work objectives are essential to success. Since it's impossible to predict what will really happen, flexibility is essential and focus critical. Knowing the trends and having determined ahead of time what types of things are likely will take care of 80-90% of the problems.

Centralized coordination is also essential to the success of this response program. There are two principles that should be followed when planning out the security strategy and particularly the response program. **Central coordination**, like a war room, works because there is a central point for all information, updates and critical decisions. However, centralized *implementation* often does not work well in my opinion. Centralized security decisions either create unnecessary security measures which are in turn rejected by the group, or miss relevant threats by not understanding the assets at hand. Instead, the **distribution** of authority about what gets secured puts responsibility on the asset owners.

The Bottom Line on Response

When planning, plan well, involve asset owners, and prioritize, predicting what really is possible and what is likely. Assess risk from an asset standpoint and respond with mitigation to avoid bigger, more costly problems down the road.

Centrally coordinate the effort and respond. Practice, and make sure plans are simple to execute and well understood at the objectives level. Engage all levels of management and clarify the protocol of getting more senior people involved so that perpetrators are not able to take advantage of the system through social engineering. Educate, educate, educate, and continue to educate the users so that they understand what is valuable, what represents risk, and how to handle data and threats.

When response is needed to an actual attack, work towards prosecution when possible. Don't let perpetrators get away with computer crime.

Effective Response

Your company needs a Computer Incident Response Team, or CIRT. Incident handling is like first aid. The response is called for after an emergency situation occurs and lives, or at least significant costs, are at stake. Expert computer response teams, like paramedics and "first responders," use carefully planned protocols that have been studied and rehearsed to provide a swift and effective response to an unexpected situation. You may not have all of the expertise in house, if not you should be partnering with an outside consulting firm that does. Either way, you're involved.

There are some guidelines here presented at a management level to help in determining where to start. Just remember that this isn't a comprehensive guide on emergency response. Rather, I've provided some guidelines to give asset owners a non-technical overview of what should be happening when mitigation and initial response have failed and data has been compromised. The following steps are found in many publications. They may be called different things, but in general, these are the steps outlined by most security professionals.

Step 1 – Effective Preparation: Effective preparation involves having a well documented policy along with standards that govern the systems and data you use every day to run the business. Involve asset owners to ensure these policies are not theoretical, but meaningful and clear, and can be understood and communicated to those that use and create digital assets. It's important to have departmental contributors signed up that stay current through education and practice sessions, and who will be ready if an event occurs. Communication protocols should be established for working with senior management (especially on weekends and after-hours), law enforcement, systems administrators and especially the media.

Step 2 – Incident Identification – When an incident alarm is triggered or spotted, someone must be responsible for making the initial call as to whether or not an actual problem exists. This individual decides if the team will work to get the system back into service, or if steps will be taken to maintain evidence that will be admissible in a court of law. This is a critical moment in the response process and should not be taken lightly. The asset owner needs to be involved as well. This is where centralized coordination moves into action, the team is notified and perhaps law enforcement officials are brought into the picture.

Step 3 – Containing the Incident – Your emergency response team is made up of IT associates as well as departmental constituents. The team is brought together initially to review the situation, determine the extent of the damage and to help the company maintain a low profile as you work through an assessment of damages. The goal is to keep the business running while keeping damages to a minimum, all the while trying to maintain any chain of evidence that may be necessary if a crime has indeed been committed. This may involve steps such as changing passwords, taking a system off line, and a determination on whether to continue operations with certain applications.

Step 4 – Eradication – This means to root out and eliminate the problem. The team at this stage is working to figure out what actually caused the problem. Is there a break-in, are there internal and external components, or is this simply the result of an error or mistake? The team works to shore up its defense against the determined cause and check for further vulnerabilities. Is this an attempt to distract the organization's defenses while something much greater is happening? Or is there something that needs to be done to strengthen the company against further attack? This includes analysis and mitigation against any weaknesses that exist. The final step is determining if there is a way to recover any lost data, or move the company back into production if a disruption has occurred.

Step 5 – Recovery – Restoration comes next. Your company has contained the incident, made assessments and deployed any additional safeguards before doing this. Hopefully steps have been taken to preserve any evidence if a crime has in fact been committed. The system is validated and inspected to ensure that there are no lingering intruders, and a process of monitoring is put in place to ensure that secure operations are in place.

Step 6 – Reporting – An incident report should be maintained, detailing what happened and the response and recovery efforts.

These steps form a simple, yet effective, structure that requires a little preplanning, the identification of people, and some ongoing training with minimal time spent staying abreast of current security trends and security measures. My advice is don't wait until there is an incident – develop a culture of response and a mindset that is always thinking, "People are getting" and looking to find out where.

Building the response mindset is essential to the completion of your security program. Start by getting the CIRT team figured out, then begin building a process of communication. Executives must understand where they come in, where other types of asset owners come in, and when and how communications take place on weekends, holidays and in the middle of the night. With this in mind we can begin working on our next mindset – one of constantly asking questions and assessing the level of risk and protection.

Dave Stelzl

Chapter 11

Mindset #6: Always Assessing

New security strategies aren't really tested. How does one develop a new security tool or technology and then test it? Bypassing a new technology isn't hard, and security can always be negated by social engineering.

Regardless of the security your company has, it can be broken, so the question is always, "Can you detect and respond before data is compromised?" There must be controls in place to ferret out this type of activity, just as accounting uses auditing to uncover unethical practices. The mindset of constantly checking is essential to security.

The Traditional Mindset

In the traditional model of security, risk is periodically measured by performing some type of assessment. Most commonly this is done through a vulnerability assessment, penetration test or both. So let's look at both.

The Vulnerability Assessment

This is easier than the penetration test and frequently less expensive, given the scope. Since the scope can be large or small, we'll focus on what I generally see delivered by commercial market-focused solution providers and security consultants.

The biggest problem is this test is scaled down to control cost, and therefore not comprehensive. When the scope is paired down, the team may review systems or networks, or perhaps the perimeter. They look for vulnerabilities or weaknesses in the protective layer of security, and of course a good team always finds them. A list of common findings may include:

- Inadequate policies that aren't read or signed off by data users.
- Remote access that isn't secure – providing no control over remote systems. (end nodes).
- Home systems used for work, not controlled by IT.
- Personal mobile devices containing email and attachments.
- ID management not centrally managed, using outdated and mismanaged passwords.
- Patching not up to date.
- Weak passwords.
- No division of responsibility on IT security staff.
- Backdoors to ease administration of servers.

The list goes on, and it is amazing how similar almost every company's list is. I tell security consultants, they could do these assessment for a lot less money if they made more predications and then just validated them rather than try to uncover every single issue. There are often too many to count, and perhaps 80% of the problem could be addressed just by taking care of the obvious issues.

Once the study is complete, it is written up. A typical report might address various areas of the technology infrastructure listing vulnerabilities with reports generated by assessment tools. Categories might include servers, network, perimeter and application. A coding scheme will then be used to signify how critical it is. (Eg. Green, yellow, red.)

This report is then delivered to the company, maybe to the CIO or CSO, but it is written in technical language for technical people, using a format that is generally hard to follow. And so it is handed to the IT personnel – perhaps the security engineers, to interpret. The engineers in turn place it on their desk, hoping to flip through it one day, but the font is small, the page count large, and in general it is not very interesting. If they were at all involved in the assessment, they will have what they care about in verbal form and will make some configuration changes. They may even ask for approval on some new technology that will then go through the normal budgeting cycle and may one day be approved.

This report is not all that useful. It's like asking for an assessment on your health that focused solely on vulnerabilities – what could go wrong with some aspect of your physical health? It would be a long report, hard to read, and somewhat useless. It might even contain numerous esoteric Latin root words. You wouldn't really have a picture of what steps to take and why, so I bet you'd put it on the shelf and go back to life as usual.

The Penetration Test

A favorite of the more serious security professionals is the pen test (short for penetration test). The consultant gets a chance at breaking in, except it's been approved so its legal. This can shake up senior managers if they thought their data was secure.

A good hacker (the security professional in this case) will always get in, especially if the company allows the use of social engineering. Some favorite tactics include dropping USB drives (flash drives) in the parking lot or inside the building. When someone finds a new one, they rejoice over the ability to take data home without having to buy one. They insert it, download all their work and the hacker wins. The hacker will then capture some data using the Trojan program that was previously installed on the flash drive, just waiting for an unsuspecting end-user to find it. The captured data becomes a trophy of this operation and is presented back as evidence of lacking security practices. The system has been broken.

Other than waking up senior managers, there is little value in this expensive service. If every system can be broken into, why spend thousands of dollars just to prove the obvious? If social engineering is not allowed, it may take longer, but the hired hackers will still eventually break in. If they don't, you just proved that your security consulting group should be replaced. On the other hand, unless you are hiring real hackers to solve your security problems, these people are not really hacking anyway, they are simply running scripts that some other hacker wrote.

I'd advise skipping the pen test unless you just want to have fun and have extra money sitting around. It's only necessary if you need to convince other executives that the company is not really secure.

Security Audit

Audits are the third type of assessment; one that may conflict with most security purchases if performed by you local system integrator. Can a company hire consultants to assess their security when the same consultant is selling security technology to them? Audits need be viewed differently and separately from an assessment conducted by a company who wants to sell you its products.

What I am calling an audit is something performed by people hired to inspect in the same way an accounting system gets audited. People look for mistakes, theft, broken security policies and more, using a set of required standards to see if you pass the test. If your system fails, the auditor provides a report on noncompliant areas.

Technology consultants who provide security services should refrain from getting involved in audits. Your organization should look to independent, unbiased companies when it comes to an audit. However, that said, the asset focused risk assessment should be seen as different.

Asset Focused Security Assesses Risk

The asset mindset is focused on constantly measuring risk associated with the loss or misuse of digital assets. At the heart of detection is finding or stopping things before they ever happen. The asset focused risk assessment is exactly that – a process to detect attacks by predicting what may happen, long before it ever does. Spending more time and money on intelligence and investigation is far more cost effective than spending the money on response and recovery following an actual attack. This mean to figure out, before attackers show up, what might happen, where the weak links are and to create the proper defense proactively.

I will talk more about how to do this in the last section of the book. Here I aim to explore the assessment mindset.

When security is viewed as a technology problem, the assessment is turned into a vulnerability assessment. This is because technical mindsets are focused on misconfigured systems, improperly written software and techniques that can be used to take advantage of weaknesses in a systems defense. This is wrong thinking that won't protect data.

The Asset mindset considers the relevant threats and constantly looks at the weak links, not only in technology but in the procedures of daily asset creation and usage. The mindset says not to trust anyone, including the end-user. The end-user is not necessarily a criminal, but mistakes are made, especially when people are not educated. So I am not advocating building a culture of mistrust.

Building a culture that accepts the idea that people are helpful, but able to ask questions is important. An example of this not working is at the airport, where I'm asked for ID. I have to pull it out of my wallet, unpack my things, and undress in public. I am convinced that they can't check all the necessary things and so have built a system without really understanding what makes something secure.

Measuring Risk

Risk is a measurement of impact and likelihood, which I've discussed. Understanding the impact of loss, or how it will affect a certain function, person, set of people, or even the entire company is important. Seemingly innocuous data often has more to do with security breaches than one might expect.

For instance, I mentioned how hackers use social engineering, and it's the innocuous data that gets them in, allowing them to pose as managers, IT workers, store clerks, or whatever they need to be. If I call you at work and know your office locations, names of your superiors, names of key projects and perhaps server names, it may be easy for you to think that I just joined your current project. Then I may be able to convince you, or one of your employees, to give me the next piece of the puzzle. This is often a building process, where the intruder gathers information until they have enough to actually ask for access. They're in. Now what will be the impact of this breech? This shows why company data must be kept confidential even when it seems like public information.

Using Assessments to Budget Spending

The first step in planning and budgeting for security should be an assessment. Analysts have used assessments for decades to plan budgets, but not every assessment provides wise guidance for departmental spending. A proper assessment will help your company avoid budgeting for new hardware developments and complicated technology. Further, a small assessment is easy to approve without going to the board. Once in motion, justification can be established for the right investments.

Let's take a look at how assessments are conducted and what constitutes a strong business case for moving relevant security projects forward. While it is not within the scope of this book to explain the full assessment process and deliverables, it's important to differentiate it from routine vulnerability assessments frequently delivered to the IT organization.

When I was working with the small bank referenced in Chapter 5, the executive VP asked me for my recommendation on where his company should go after the first meeting; toward the end of my house analogy. How could he move from a protection-only strategy to the PDR model I described? I recommended an assessment. Then it occurred to me he might have already conducted one. Likely, your company has also done this.

Risk Assessment

While many reports are called risk assessments, few offer any measurement of risk (the measure of impact versus the likelihood that something bad will happen). Certainly, there are more complete definitions that take into consideration business impact (quantitative and qualitative measurements of downtime and disruption), annual rates of expectancy and other risk-related factors. But the goal here is not to build your security assessment process, but to build the mindset. The risk-assessment process creates the justification required to move the program forward.

Rather than delivering a heavyweight document and paying a consultant by the pound, you hope to receive a fairly simple and relevant document. Must be written in such a way as to help data owners in your organization understand where they are at risk, which threats are relevant, and where they should apply their dollars so it actually benefits the security relevant to their business requirements.

Here's a simple formula to follow:

- *Focus on assets.* Remember Question 1: "What are you trying to protect?" This question was created to move the conversation away from technology and toward assets. Now that you've identified the asset and successfully transitioned your attention from the technology to digital assets, it will be important to keep it there. Write the report specifically with this focus in mind, and then supporting data can be delivered to the technical team.

- *Address the entire system.* Traditional security assessments focus on perimeter issues, inside or outside security controls, or perhaps the entire enterprise. This risk assessment should include the servers, networks and connectivity associated with a particular set of assets—something tightly defined that can be accomplished in a short amount of time, but will have great impact. Remember to include the people who create, use, and modify data within the company along with any third-party companies that process data or are subcontracted by your organization. The set of assets being assessed will encompass all relevant trusted systems, all points of access, policies, procedures and anything that may affect the given system. I'm not saying you must assess the entire organization, rather take some of the key systems and address all relevant aspects. At some point you want to address the entire company, however making this process too big often causes companies to ignore the requirement to make this a continuous process. Perhaps thinking about it at a departmental level would be helpful.

- *Focus on business processes.* Look at asset loss or compromise. Business processes and critical systems, including security controls, change control, users and data sources become relevant to assessing the likelihood of data loss, integrity loss or data availability.

- *Consider relevant threats.* There are numerous issues with every system, so relevancy is important. Over time, relevancy will change with business climate, data age, market conditions, employee turnover and innovation. When you have a health exam, you don't want a list of every potential issue or every disease known to mankind. Rather, you want to know if you face any immediate dangers. The same is true in a business risk assessment. You're looking for immediate danger.

- **Prioritize according to business impact.** End-users and managers must be included in the process of measuring the importance of the systems involved, but it's up to the data owner to prioritize the issues based on impact and likelihood.

- **Deliver measurable risk.** Data owners value something they can understand such as a graph. The assessment team must have a documented methodology and justification for their findings. The deliverable here is simple: an executive level risk graph with some explanation.

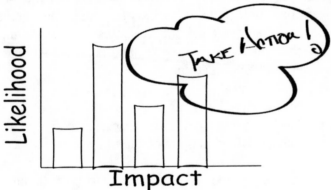

- **Create a continuous process.** This may be the most important point on this list. Performing a one-time assessment raises awareness, but quarterly updates allow you to manage the remediation process. If only one assessment is done, or they are carried out only once a year, your picture of risk will be tainted. Providing an initial baseline and then adding quarterly updates allows you to review new projects, system changes, and future plans to identify issues and concerns. At the same time, you have the opportunity to remind users and managers of the potential dangers, help them plan continuously and follow the prescribed roadmap toward securing data. Without this last step, you will likely lose your momentum in building a successful security strategy.

Using the Risk Assessment

Information Security companies sell risk assessments, claiming they provide an unbiased look at the given company's systems. Many have asked whether or not a single company can both perform this assessment and provide the remediation services.

The answer is an emphatic yes. Security consulting companies can use an unbiased process that takes into consideration certain technologies they understand. These companies depend on their security expertise as it pertains to specific technology areas. It's actually a smart strategy. The conflict shows up when companies that sell technology also provide audits. Audits and risk assessments are not the same thing.

You want people who really understand the technology to be evaluating it, and they may be the best ones to integrate security into it. Just make sure they really understand the security side.

Consider the alarm salesperson who comes to your home, walks through your halls, garage and around the back of the house, and then points out the security holes. He shows you how easy it is to break in by basically performing a free assessment. If he is really good at what he does, he will show you that your home is not secure through protection strategies such as locked doors and windows. He has essentially become your trusted advisor because he understands how his product is built and where it is going to fit best. He makes recommendations based upon the impact of an intrusion and shows ways to reduce the likelihood of an attack. Your only consideration at this point is the trustworthiness of the individual. Make sure your consultant is honest and you will do well.

It would be rare to hire a home security firm that doesn't sell any security systems. You look to the manufacturer or value-added reseller to understand the risks, what their products offer, and then you ask them to perform the installation.

In the corporate world, this entire process may be done in cooperation with IT or overseen by the security staff. An assessment is not an audit in this case, but a process from conception to implementation, and all the way to an ongoing security program. A thorough job will measure risk, configure changes, possibly recommend some new product requirements, user awareness training, and some changes to current procedures. An ongoing process will then be established to maintain this program. If it doesn't make sense to build this in-house, then consider some form of outsourced monitoring.

Delivering Results to the Data Owner

The critical factor in everything I've discussed is in the deliverable. Once you have agreed on an assessment process that measures risk, reporting must remain at the data-owner level. This means technical people perform the information-gathering at the technical levels, deliver technical assessment materials and are available to explain their findings. But higher level people need to be involved to review data assets and risk at the business level, consider technical findings and then provide management level reporting that makes sense to the people driving the business. This won't be a technical document, but rather a risk document that can be used to make strategic decisions and budgetary planning.

I recommend involving your higher-level consultants at the business level to understand the applications, data value, impact and likelihood of things going bad. Your primary deliverable is written with the data owner and other corporate executives in mind, using charts, pictures and bullet points to communicate clearly and quickly what is needed to reduce exposure. If you don't have these people on staff, you would do well to form a relationship with a company that can do this quickly and efficiently, at a reasonable cost.

Note: Security assessments like these do not need to take months or cost hundreds of thousands of dollars. Many of the issues are the same across companies in your industry. A consultant that does this for a living can often predict, before ever setting foot in your office, what some of the major issues are based on current threats and practices. Hire someone who is willing to admit this, perform assessments quickly and with some frequency.

Formal presentations are then used to explain the findings and recommend action steps. Don't bother spending the time on business cost analysis unless you have a real need for this data. A roadmap can paint a picture of how the enterprise may be extended to new markets where computing is unsafe, if necessary. This may include accessing intranet portals and email from the local coffee shop.

The Ongoing Remediation Program

View this as a phased and ongoing program—a roadmap. Most companies should not purchase large security remediation projects the day after receiving the findings. The results will often be overwhelming, so instead set a roadmap that can be followed over time, built into new projects and made a part of any new initiative. Focus on the urgent issues upfront.

This assessment process gives you control over future project initiatives. Quarterly updates will get this information back in front of people who are handling and creating data, so that every member of the organization is constantly reminded of the risks associated with creation, use and disposal of data and systems. It must become part of the corporate culture if data is going to be secure. This will result in the frequent review of security dealing with new projects and system changes that affect the overall security architecture and represent new levels of risk. At the same time, you are reminded of the exposure you already have without these remediation efforts.

If done properly, assessors will be invited to planning sessions, company meetings and strategy sessions to consider how new initiatives change the risk equation.

Each quarter, you should contract to update what you have and expand your view. Every project, system change, or application addition or enhancement is potentially an increase in the scope of your security program. Updates represent reminders of the progress toward remediation, while scope changes come with new projects. Doing this on a scheduled basis will simplify it and ultimately cost you less in time and money

Here's the bottom line: Use this process to expand your view of security within the organization, and deliver greater value to company management and end-user groups that interact with your assets.

The job of security is to maintain data availability, confidentiality and integrity on any part of the company's infrastructure. This is not just pure security technology which belongs to a special group called IT Security. It touches every aspect of creating, using, transmitting, storing, archiving and disposing of mission-critical corporate data assets.

With this new knowledge, you're ready to build the final mindset, a holistic mindset. As you go through the assessment process, you'll find a holistic mindset provides a framework for building the right security controls into whatever aspect of the company you manage.

Chapter 12

Mindset #7: Holistic

Security, if treated as a technology problem that focuses solely on protection, is a like a point without any dimensions. Introducing detection and response to create a PDR model creates a line – a two dimensional model that only has length and width. But when we add administrative and physical aspects, a matrix is formed with both length, width, and also depth. It gives us a three dimensional model covering nine boxes, each containing depth that will backup failed security processes. Companies can use this model to protect the assets they depend on to stay in business.

The nine box model covers interrelated aspects of security, including disaster recovery, business continuity, training and user awareness, and even the physical aspects of data center security and building security. When the firewall team is asked to secure the data, they are handed a task they cannot accomplish. All they can do is block certain types of unauthorized traffic. Once that data leaves the building on mobile devices or through email to a home computer, IT is powerless to secure it.

	Protection	Detection	Response
Administrative	Policy		BCP/DR
Technical	Firewall	Intrusion Detection	
Physical		Camera	Police

Note: I have intentionally left this model incomplete because it has so many variations. One model will not fit every company.

The holistic mindset recognizes that the data owner understands, more than others, the changing value of their data and can best discuss the relevant changing nature of threats. While this person does not necessarily have a technical view of the threat landscape, a qualified technical person will be able to translate the data owner's viewpoint into technology choices. Other aspects of the security program may be driven through other departments, coordinated by the security officer and compliance officers, depending on the size and type of organization.

The Traditional Mindset

Traditional security is made of individual boxes. In smaller companies, IT departments are saddled with the responsibility to maintain and secure systems. Very large companies may have different teams that focus on firewalls, intrusion detection systems or desktop security. In both cases, security is largely a technology problem, left to technologists to solve using technology. Both approaches are destined to fail because they leave out the weak links, the data owners and users, and these methods attempt to centralize security decisions. The best security is determined at the departmental level, and then managed centrally, and responded to through centralized coordination with distributed involvement.

Asset Focused Security is Holistic

Asset focused security is holistic and considers far more than just the technology. The security strategy considers the people, environment, types of data and systems, usage requirements, and many other aspects.. Technology is a part of the solution as automation is used to boost security levels and take on tasks that cannot easily be performed by humans.

A security software executive recently told me, "The more people involved, the greater the risk. Companies focus their employees on getting the job done, not securing the data." There seems to be a much higher security awareness when workers are dealing with cash. Once we turn to digital assets, the value is no longer apparent and the risk increases dramatically.

The holistic security model must consider all angles. Data will be created by end-user departments, then passed through the hands of various user groups, and some users will work from home while others travel. Many will use portable computers of various forms to handle the data, some personally owned and lacking any real security.

Administrative Security

The holistic security matrix starts with administrative security where policies that govern data are set. Unless dictated by an upcoming audit, policy is never a pressing issue, and so it is rarely established up front. Policies, however, do two things:

- Drive the security architecture
- Limit the company's liability

You will need to consult your lawyer to make sure liability is fully covered. Policies demonstrate to a court of law that your company does not allow certain activities. If one employee offends another with an act against policy, the company is protected. The same is true when data is compromised, misused or stolen through an act against policy.

For instance, imagine that one of your employees is viewing website material which is offensive to another employee, or is sending out some type of protest or discriminating email. Both of these actions may cause another employee to file a lawsuit. You will need to demonstrate that all employees are required to read and sign off on an appropriate computer use policy that prohibits this type of activity.

Another frequent scenario occurs when company systems are used for personal use. It might be hard to legally defend a policy stating that employees can't use their systems for anything personal The alternative is to state that all systems are owned by the company and are subject to audit, and that all email and other forms of communication are considered the property of your company, and you maintain the right to monitor email activity and other communications. That is why call centers frequently state that the call may be monitored. It's only for training purposes if the company finds there is a problem. Then they can go back, listen to the call, and take action which will result in some form of training, including termination as an example to others.

Administrative security also provides the procedures on how data is handled. They direct data creators to classify data, guide custodians through the process of administering data, access control and maintenance. These documents detail how systems are to be protected, what technologies are approved for use, and will limit the use of certain technologies that might present vulnerabilities to the security architecture.

Finally, administrative security provides guidelines, or areas that are not necessarily binding, but highly recommended.

Procedures will also provide a response plan. Documents such as disaster recovery plans should be considered as part of the security strategy. Procedures that are used in the event of a compromise or disaster must be well documented, understood by data owners, users and custodians. They should be well rehearsed to ensure that the response time meets the minimum requirements. Many disaster recovery efforts have failed simply because no one ever tested them. It's important that backup tapes actually work, and a restore can be performed in the required time frame.

Technical Security

Technical security is often given the most attention, yet there is still a major flaw in the security design at this level because companies are not able to detect and respond. The technology aspects require input from the data owners. IT personnel can only put the right technology in place when the data owner has understood the impact vs. likelihood or risk level the company has.

I helped a medical services company who hired a third party to review the risks associated with this organization's current computing practices. The risk report revealed significant problems such as storage systems tied to their main applications that were nearly full. A proposal was given to fix the major issues, but the data owner delegated this review process to IT. The budget allocated didn't cover the need, and the data owners were unwilling to be involved. So IT was left to figure out what needed to be done based on a budget that had been set prior to the assessment. This approach is destined to fail. Further, when it does fail, it will be considered IT's fault.

The holistic model incorporates technical security designed with the data in mind, and policies are developed according to the value and risk associated with the type of information the company creates, stores and uses. So, as we discussed in the previous section on due care, the technology is chosen because it represents reasonable steps of securing data.

The technology choices provide an integrated approach to securing the data. The asset mindset looks for technology that provides a more seamless, easy to manage solution. It may even be built right into the networks, systems or operating systems – something that may create conflict across division lines in the technology support areas, but this is the future of effective security choices.

Physical Security

The final area is physical security. In most organizations, it resides in a completely different area from technical security. This isn't all bad, except that each group designs their own security in a vacuum. There isn't much cooperation between these groups because no one sees the connection between the two.

Even if it seems hacking is unrelated to physical security, nothing could be farther from the truth.

By understanding the assets, relevant threats, and how social engineering works, physical security personnel will be able to build a more effective security strategy. It's not just physical intruders threatening the company. Sometimes I get the feeling that physical security personnel think they are primarily watching for some major break in, a riot or an employee going crazy. This might happen, but what about the more subtle break in, where someone comes in and plants software on a system and then accesses computers through the Internet.

Companies need a process for when authorized people show up at odd hours or people forget their badge. They might claim that they just need something from their cube, and they have credentials back in the car. For some reason, security personnel believe people when they offer to retrieve their badge from their car, and even allow them in without the badge.

Directory systems with pictures are great for this sort of thing, as well as badges that tie to computer access control. This means I have to have a badge to get into my system, and if I forget it, the guard can't be nice and let me in. It's now out of their control.

Physical security must be designed not only to protect the physical plant, but also the data. This is done when data owners review the overall picture with security savvy people who help sketch out a high level plan for administrative, technical and physical security. The details can then be developed by smaller groups with a greater level of expertise in the area they are working on.

Creating the Holistic Mindset

Creating this holistic mindset is not easy. There needs to be cooperation between business and technical people, users and administrators, and physical security personnel.

If you use my 7 mindsets, the overall security program becomes a company-wide effort of securing digital assets. The company becomes aware of what these assets are, what kinds of threats are relevant to your industry, and how likely an attack or breach is, both from the inside and outside.

Dave Stelzl

Part Three

Dave Stelzl

Chapter 13
Applying Security

As a manager or executive, how will you apply the mindsets we've covered and build your asset security strategy?

In **The Fifth Discipline,** *author Peter Senge states that people will die for a well-formed vision. When they understand current realities, see the possibilities of what could be and believe in their advisors' ability to take them there, they'll make the journey.*

Successful people surround themselves with experts of all kinds to make sure they are well informed before making decisions. Likewise, wise security decisions are made using the justification and guidance brought through the assessment process described in the last chapter.

Everything starts with a new understanding of the risks involved in running a business dependent on mission-critical assets. This is not a technical issue. As the asset owner, you agree that threats are changing; protection, detection and response are necessary to the security architecture.

An assessment shows, based on provided impact data, the likelihood of a breach. This information is then used to help prioritize certain systems in terms of risk. Now I'll provide guidance to you as the person liable for losses.

Interpreting the Risk Assessment

Over the last two years, I've asked many security professionals—from product manufacturers, software developers, solution providers, security boutiques, large integrators, and smaller mid-market and SMB solution providers/resellers—where they find the greatest vulnerabilities in the corporate security strategies they see. Where are the big holes in the average security architecture? Here's what they said:

Policy. While most companies have a security policy, many do not update it on a regular basis. Employees may be required to read it, but tracking is inadequate, and the average policy lacks the supporting standards, guidelines and procedures. Across the board, policies lack enforcement, reducing them to a set of guidelines. They don't necessarily limit liability and drive architecture, as they're designed to do.

Segmentation. Internal networks are treated as one big trusted family. Regardless of data sensitivity and regulatory requirements like HIPAA or GLBA, companies have failed to segment divisions that require different degrees of security. Even with voice networks —a logical part of the design—companies have been remiss and/or noncompliant. One of the best examples is higher education where administrative and financial systems are on the same network as faculty and student records. These are three groups, requiring three very different levels of security, but they're all in one segment, separated only by passwords.

Applications. Web applications are particularly deficient when it comes to security. While there are application testing tools from companies like HP, as well as application-specific firewalls, many companies aren't using them, and they don't require security to be built into the application. Third-party application developers have told me it's just too costly and time-consuming to put security into the application. They recommend that clients ensure a safe environment by using firewalls and other security devices. This is unbelievable and unacceptable. Don't allow third party developers to program with this mindset. They will expose your assets before you know what happened.

IP-Telephony. This application may be the creator and transmitter of some of the most critical information in the organization. This is where companies handle mergers and acquisitions, stock trades, employee decisions, changes to key products and new ideas—in short, the future of the organization. Why do so many companies assume this is a safe place to create and transmit highly sensitive information? Every phone system should be seen as another computer with access to key information. Make sure your installers understand security.

In general, default configurations are not secure even if they claim that the security is built in. Ask them if the full version of security software is present in the system, or if it's a "skinnied down" version. Often it's there to look good rather than to provide the security you need.

System Security. Large servers are connected to web applications, allowing customers, internal and external users, and anyone else to create or interact with data. Assessments have shown system security is generally weak, granting users complete access (including creation, read, write and deletion rights) to key data. Passwords may allow guest access and user IDs often remain active after employees are gone. As jobs change and needs evolve, users' access rights often become out of step with their needs. Some administrators create back doors or trusted relationships among systems to ease their burden, but wind up creating significant weaknesses in the security architecture. While there are a lot of technologies here, data owners must be aware of the procedures used to secure data on the servers.

Remote Access. Remote access always seems to be a problem. Workstations and PDAs access mission-critical data from just about anywhere, day and night. Systems used at home by children and spouses for chatting, blogging, shopping and other recreations are then used to access corporate systems. Laptops are accessing these same systems from airports, hotels, coffee shops and public hotspots without any concern for privacy. Simple passwords, POP3 protocols (used for mail on many mobile systems), webmail and instant-message applications are used to transmit highly sensitive information in the clear. Messaging is one of the big black holes out there in security and it should be seen as an open door that needs special consideration.

Portable Data Systems. Another laptop/PDA problem exists when we consider the safety of data as it leaves the enterprise. A recent *USA Today* article described how a company performed a study on data security and mobile devices. After purchasing 10 cell phones from eBay, the firm showed how carelessly people dispose of data. With some Internet and homegrown tools, they were able to recover enough information to print an eight-foot stack of 8.5" by 11" documents of Social Security numbers, account numbers, credit card information, sales efforts, and merger and acquisition information from text-message sessions. In most cases, the phones had been erased, yet the data was recoverable. Every company has these devices – do you know what data is being transmitted and stored on them? More importantly do you have some guidelines on a disposal process for these devices?

Wireless. Despite the endless stories about wardriving, people still opt for the ease of unencrypted wireless access. Other wireless networks may have been encrypted using the WEP protocol, but never updated. This takes about 15 minutes to break according to my security colleagues. Many voice applications now use wireless. With a simple tool downloaded from the Internet, these wireless networks are easily compromised. People use them without realizing how insecure they are. We need the convenience of wireless computing, but prudence demands a higher level of security, including more detection and response through some centralized management process.

Partners, Guests and Contractors. While many companies have managed to secure the perimeter, back-door connections are often created to allow partners to share applications. Routers connect seemingly secure networks to other companies that may have lower security standards. Guests are provided full access to the network, with only a password standing between them and sensitive data. Third-party contractors often have access to systems they maintain, with full administrative rights and no accountability.

Real-Life Situations

My own findings support the problems I've just identified. I recently received payment from a major global company through the Internet. I was sitting in an airport, accessing an insecure email account and one of my messages contained this client's credit card, security code and expiration date.

In a recent travel booking experience, I contacted the concierge to book my limo from the airport. He asked that I fill out a form to provide flight information along with schedules and payment terms. When he sent me the form to fill out (an unencrypted Microsoft Word document), imagine my surprise when I opened the document only to find out that he had sent me someone else's form, already filled out. The form contained their name, address, credit card number and expiration date. I immediately called the concierge back, letting him know what he had sent me. He apologized for not deleting the information first. It sounded like he thought I might be complaining about the extra work involved in having to delete this information myself. I am convinced that he did not understand what he had done.

Another time, I was assessing a telecommunication company's security. The IT group had actually created segments going around the firewall to allow one of its applications to work correctly. It was a temporary solution, but it had been in place for more than a month.

One of my clients calls on a major software manufacturer that processes accounting data for small companies throughout the United States. A recent firewall issue threatened to shut down his software application, so the firewall manufacturer actually recommended that he pull out the firewalls temporarily and use access control lists in his routers until the problem could be solved. It's been more than a month since he implemented this temporary fix, and these accounts hold all kinds of information that could be used by cyberthieves to create new identities or apply for loans, among other risks.

Another client was donating PCs to charity without deleting data. He was erasing the disks, but studies show it's relatively easy to recover data from an erased disk.

While working with a regional bank, I discovered its primary banking applications provided complete access to third-party processing companies. They had rights to not only read information, but to change or delete it. This bank also transmits account information across the Internet as part of its loan approval process—clearly a violation of GLBA.

I could go on, but you get my point. Security is weak, and much of the problem can be fixed by education without getting into highly technical details. The data users are often the ones creating the greatest exposure while IT is saddled with the major responsibility, and there is little communication between the two parties.

The Product List

When an assessment reveals these kinds of issues, companies often receive a list of needed products from IT or a local technology company. You shouldn't view it as a product list, but as a component list.

One of my friends purchases and restores historical homes. When I first entered the last home he purchased—a 100-year-old house in South Carolina—I was amazed at the amount of work he faced, especially with the electrical systems. With holes in the walls and missing light fixtures, I could see the wiring wouldn't meet state codes. I imagined what would happen if someone stood in a puddle of water and turned on a faulty appliance—a disaster waiting to happen.

As an educated homeowner and handyman, his first thought was to assess the situation by crawling through and inspecting every part of the system. He made a list with numerous components to choose from to create a safe living environment.

You should view your component list in the same way. Don't call them solutions, because they're not. Don't think of them as products to install that will create a secure computing environment. The idea of components carries the right connotation, instilling the idea that a group of products/integration, policies and education are required to create a safe computing environment. In fact, all nine boxes of the coverage model presented in section 2 should be considered as one seamless system or security architecture. Training those that create and manage assets on the business side is the glue that holds all of this together.

Remote-Access Example

We've all used VPNs (Virtual Private Networks that provide remote access to corporate servers while traveling or working from home). Let's assume that you want to provide or have secure remote access to applications you use every day. A technical person may ask how many ports are needed, how many users will use the system, and which applications the user is planning to access. These questions push security decisions down to the security team, which is not the place we want to start. This centralizes the initial security planning rather than getting the asset owner involved.

Let's try another approach. As the asset owner, ask: "What are we trying to protect?" We can assume we need to access certain key systems remotely, but it can actually be done without the aid of a VPN. The VPN was introduced to provide some level of security. What does the VPN actually provide? Your first thought may be secure remote access, but does it accomplish this? Your second answer may be encryption of data between the endpoint and perimeter. This answer is correct, but how secure is it?

The fact is, encrypting data may make systems less secure. Of course, I'm exaggerating a bit to make my point. But because data cannot be seen, whatever is happening on an end-node is passing through the perimeter—perhaps to a DMZ (Demilitarized zone) area on the network, but through the firewall, without the ability to see what's coming in. In fact, many cyberthieves encrypt attack software to avoid inspection as it passes through your security lines of defense.

The solution is to add something to this picture. When you know what needs to be protected, you have the information needed to start designing a more secure way to access data remotely. We may add some way to authenticate users with strong or two-factor authentication. A token or one-time password could be used.

Secondly, we should add some way to ensure end users' workstations have the right patches, are running the latest software versions and meet workstation configuration standards. We can do this with a network access control server that inspects end-user systems for proper updates and configurations.

It would be helpful to have some level of intrusion-prevention software running at the perimeter where data is deciphered, ensuring malicious traffic doesn't enter the corporation's trusted network. And don't forget you need a way to monitor activity: when users come in, who they are, what they do and when they leave. Accountability is important here. Is there real-time monitoring and alerting, as well as an audit trail? This defines the detection part of the security equation.

At the end-node, the operating system must be protected from all forms of malware, spyware and misuse. Several applications may be required to do this, and the end-user may have much of this in place. The security solution is incomplete without asking these questions and addressing the issues listed above. Notice we didn't get rid of the VPN but added some things to make this situation secure.

Wireless Application

When using wireless applications, the end users must be clean, authenticated, authorized and permitted. Once connected, they must be monitored.

You will need some way to keep the end-node safe from malware and remote-control attacks by using antivirus, anti-spyware and perhaps some form of intrusion-prevention software. There's steps to take when using an asset mind set. Your corporate network first assesses the end-node's condition before allowing a connection to be established, then checks with an access control server to ensure the user is authorized to come in. You then determine the restrictions that should be applied to each session. Strong authentication ensures the user is, in fact, who he claims to be.. Finally, you provide encryption and some means of centrally managing this activity. Of course all of this gets designed by the IT group and/or partners that help support your network. The difference is that your security is designed with the data in mind.

Regardless of where connection occur (internal or external, wireless, partner, consultant, guest or other), the same steps are required. Encryption may not be required in some instances, and a simple password may work for some internal users. But, in general, you should implement these basic safety controls if the user is going to achieve secure remote access, or secure access of any kind.

There's more. These technology aspects will be implemented to different degrees based on the type of data you are securing and the relevant threats. Once in place, you'll need to train those who create and access the data on how to handle data, given the security controls you've now put in place. Policies and procedures will also need to be created to help govern this. Make sure they are relevant and meaningful. Meaningless policies get shelved and become wasted effort. No one will pay attention to them.

Systems and Storage

You may have applications with servers, storage and end-user devices. Each concept should be applied to the operating systems and servers, application and database, as well as connectivity. Again, it's the same scenario of ensuring a clean system, authentication, authorization and event correlation. Encryption is applied to transmission, storage and archival.

In each case, the three pillars of security are applied: confidentiality, integrity and availability of the system and its data. In the network case, single points of failure are eliminated. In the systems and storage area, the same is true, with the added function of ensuring proper backups and restore capability.

If you're familiar with applications on servers, you recognize that tapes often fail, and system failures take far longer than the average four-hour response time to be placed back into full service. This is why Symantec bought Veritas in 2005. In its quest to secure data, operating systems and applications, it needed the capability to back up data and create a highly available configuration.

Voice Applications

In my seminars I frequently run into people using this technology. Several features make VoIP attractive, including collaboration and the combining of applications. Security should apply across this implementation, from the initial server installation to the handsets that are really undercover PCs.

When people pick up the phone, they are convinced their conversations are off the record. But the growing popularity of unified communications is not just about voice, but voice, video and email collaboration. The real time nature of this application does not mean data is safe at all. It's not unless steps are taken to secure it.

It's not that traditional analog voice applications couldn't be taped or recorded, because they can be and sometimes are. But the tools available today for network-hacking allow intruders to easily record voice along with data. Because we know bots and other malicious software products are being used across a company's infrastructure to steal information, we can be sure people are tapping into VoIP. We also know that each phone set is a PC in a sense and can be used to access data on the corporate network if not properly secured.

Companies that could be securing their voice are not. People who sell voice are not educating consumers on its risks in an effort to keep the sales moving. But this is a disservice to you as the customer. It's easy to record voice on a network—to sit between two executive callers with a PC and capture information discussed regarding future mergers, big projects, coming layoffs or the latest strategy roadmaps. You can even assume that internal people are doing this just for the fun of it.

Even some of the simplest steps aren't taken. Newer switch and router technologies are designed for voice to improve quality and give administrators the necessary security to keep an eye on their networks. Simple logging tools and centralized correlation, alerting and network time protocols ensure that logging is time-stamped properly to allow for precise correlation. In other words, your IT department needs a way to see what is going on throughout the VOIP system at all times.

Phone gateways that provide for encryption should be used where communications are sensitive. This is certainly the case in any large or mid-size organization at the executive level. Encryption can be applied to certain parts of the network, such as between the CEO's and CFO's offices. In addition, certificates or software token passwords can provide secure login at phone stations.

Phones are computers in this scenario, so it's important to guard against recording or people using this connection point to gain access to secure network resources.

IPS (Intrusion Prevention Software) is an important tool as well. While some calling applications come with scaled-down IPS software, mid-sized and enterprise-level businesses require greater protection. Without a full-blown IPS software solution, complete correlation of events is impossible. This is the key to applying the detection-response component of the security architecture. Remember: relying on protection is not good enough.

Further, it's becoming popular to build many of the security software features we see on PCs right into the network. Cisco and Juniper are heavily investing in building antivirus, anti-spyware, IPS, encryption, authentication and many other security controls into their products. They should be implemented when installing voice in any major corporation.

Finally, it has always been a best practice to lock down operating systems on servers, making sure guest access, general administrator access and OS services are kept to a minimum. This same consideration must be extended to phone systems. As these small computers that resemble phones are installed, they come with installation tools, web access and troubleshooting features that are often turned on. These systems must be locked down to ensure security. Access is possible from remote locations, exposing sensitive information to a variety of network resources.

Security can be achieved, but it takes thought and due care. Without it, your company will be exposed to serious threats and liability.

I recently asked a security engineer who specializes in voice about the top four voice insecurities. Here's the list:
- Insecure wireless/voice installations.
- Poor use of network segmentation and router configurations with voice.

- Lack of locked-down systems (meaning that devices are running services that can be exploited to gain access to the data.)
- Relying on lower-end security features rather than adding more full-featured event detection tools.

Three out of four are simple configuration issues. Only the last one requires additional products. But people don't think through the design and end up installing voice insecurely. It's only a matter of time before someone is listening in—and perhaps years before you find out. Remember: cyber-criminals are not looking to disrupt a business when they can surreptitiously seek profits. It's in their best interest if you go about business as usual.

The Final Solution

With your assessment results in hand, you can begin making the right decisions to secure data. Still, some of this may be somewhat confusing. Remember that tossing this entire project over to the security team, at this point, is a bad move. Asset owners need to be involved.

If you've completed the assessment process, you should have gone through this process with key stakeholders, asset owners, representative users and security consultants (internal or external). Your technical people should have interacted with managers, end user departments and anyone using or creating sensitive data. This entire team is critical to the solution process.

In a recent follow-up program, I was asked why companies consistently hit roadblocks, even when using these principles. I asked for a show of hands on how many people had kept the team in tact through the process. Sadly, few had. I then asked how many had put together executive level findings with business impact vs. purely technical documents. Several said they wished they had. Finally, I asked them to identify the asset owners. In most cases, the process had been delegated down to those without any substantial liability. That explains why these projects are often unsuccessful and why a follow-up is needed. You need accountability when implementing these steps, so form accountability relationships within the team. Having a non-technical project manager is the best choice—someone who will hold your feet to the fire without worrying about offending people, and with enough clout in the corporation to get things done.

Keeping Executives Involved

Always start with the assets. Highly sensitive information and a company's understanding of exposure keep everyone interested. Tie each initiative and requirements to critical processes within the enterprise. Some will be technical, suited for the technical team, but others will be at a business level and will require changes in policy and procedure.

Rather than referring to the network or servers, the project team should learn to speak in terms of intellectual capital, customer data, strategic documents and liability. Stay away from technical topics, which will be addressed in a separate meeting with your technical experts. Focus on the answers given in Question 1: What are we trying to protect?

Relevant Threats

Extending the enterprise brings new risks and exposure. A review of these areas, supported by your assessment, will help team members see where they're exposed and where changes are needed. Align your findings with the company's priorities to reach agreement and a common vision. Business threats include loss of customer confidence, market share, branding and reputation, and competitive advantage—not to mention the liability that comes with losing sensitive data.

Creating a Cultural Mindset for Security

Begin your remediation plan with the area in which you have the greatest company exposure, not with products like antivirus, workstation intrusion protection, firewall and other tools available at Staples or Best-Buy.

Don't forget about the end-user side of this project. Starting with the education of data users is likely your highest impact activity. Highlighting security that can be added to your company's existing infrastructure is a great place to start on the technical side. If you've had your infrastructure for some time, perhaps it's time to upgrade security controls that can be built in, or added systems and networks. This will ease total cost of ownership and operational expenses. Leveraging existing infrastructure and using built in security technology is almost always easier to integrate.

Take a look at core systems like the network or key servers. If your assessment reveals serious problems or even a high likelihood of being compromised, it's time to take action.

The same can be done with storage systems. Rather than looking at the desktop to secure data, start with access control, availability and integrity of data. Storage companies have been acquiring and building technology that can be integrated into their systems over the past five years to ease the burden of business continuity, access control, and data integrity or data loss. Generally this is the cost effective way to go.

Product Overview

Avoid using acronyms and esoteric technological concepts with the project team. This is not executive vernacular, so people won't understand what's being implemented. Instead, relate all diagrams to concepts and functionality. Then let the technical group figure out the details with the charter to bring back a functional plan.

For instance, software added to a client's network can process data, looking for malicious traffic and viruses. Firewall functions (a well-understood product) can be added to create segmentation within the network.

A small appliance may be added internally to create visibility into the company's systems, showing who is accessing what, when they're doing it and what they're actually doing while connected. This greatly reduces the risks associated with remote access, wireless computing and perhaps web-server interfaces. It's like setting up parent controls in your home so you know what your kids are up to on the Internet. In this case, we are managing identities.

By adding software to the remote client like a laptop or workstation, we can create a shell around the operating system that won't allow anything to execute or operate that machine without the system administrator knowing about it and the user identifying himself. This is the core of workstation based intrusion protection software agents (IPS).

Use a Roadmap, Not a Short, Expensive Project

The next steps are critical. If you don't have a roadmap, either the project will end prematurely or people will get off track spending unnecessary money on things that don't actually help the situation. Make sure the entire team is on board with the plan.

Your technical people should be equipped to bring insights to the project team. Those with a purely technical mindset can be slow to give up existing technology if it competes with new directions, politics, or takes away from earlier choices; especially when brand loyalty has been established through gifts, golf and free lunches. Gain the sponsorship from other asset owners, then reorient the team.

Evaluations may be required. If so, develop a project plan to manage the process. Don't install free products that become the de facto standard. Your goal should be proof of concept, with preset milestones and agreed-upon steps following the successful completion of predetermined objectives. Often it's cheaper to use technology for a period of time and replace it later, compared to going through months of evaluation. Many of these products are similar, so it's the design, data user education, and response plan that really make the difference here. Stick with larger manufacturers that have a complete offering. In the end, their products will integrate more easily and offer better management.

In the next chapter, I will take a look at what people are selling – not from a technical evaluation level, but rather a strategy. While your final project success is not all about technology, there are some things you should be aware of.

Chapter 14

Making Sense of Vendor Strategies

There are a million companies that offer competing security technologies, so which one do you choose? Many of the technologies we have today were created by creative people who left larger companies with a great idea, received funding through venture capital, and then reunited with their original company. This is one way new inventions come about. The larger companies then take this new concept and build it into their product set.

Most of the good technology eventually gets purchased by larger network, security and storage companies, and the integration is done for us. Take advantage of this cycle.

On the other hand, we now have several competing technology directions out there, making it difficult for managers to understand where to go.

But it turns out that these choices are not as complex as they seem. In this chapter we will take a look at some of the primary strategies out there, where they differ, where they are similar, but most important, where they matter.

Success means moving away from products, finding the assets and asset owner, and creating a culture for security within the context of your company's business model. Only after this is understood can the right products be chosen.

We compare the features and benefits of security produces to differentiate one company or product from another. We call in the engineers to argue functionality points, or we look to outside firms to bring in their security certifications, resumes, case studies and perhaps pricing. Often, it comes down to commodity products at the lowest price. This is not the way to solve a security problem.

We're acting on a preconceived notion of what we expect to see, and we're talking primarily to technologists. There are many great reasons not to burden asset owners at this point. It's become a technology issue with a technology answer, and this leads to project failure.

If you're in the middle of such a project and turned to this chapter first, welcome to the book. There are a number of factors to keep in mind when working to secure data, but they're all based on the previous chapters. My advice? Start at the beginning.

I do not intend to compare all of the technologies available or turn this book into a product recommendation list. Rather, I want to examine some of the strategies used by product manufacturers, look at the strengths and weaknesses of various models, and bring you back to the foundational principles of making wise decisions when it comes to securing assets.

Consider Recent Technology Decisions

If you've had the opportunity to work on security projects in the past, it's helpful to analyze how successful they've been. Perhaps you've convinced executives to make company-wide choices that involved liability and data assets, or you've performed an in-depth assessment that led to multiple remediation projects. More frequently, I meet people who have performed or hired people to conduct the assessment, but remediation projects did not follow. It is helpful to understand why.

Over the last year, I've talked with more than 400 consultants in the security field about significant projects they've worked on. Many were unable to come up with one that represented a total mindset change on the company's part. Those who could summon a successful example conveyed a consistent theme. They had a security vision for securing assets that involved data owners, data users, and those who manage the data. Many leveraged their senior managers or business-savvy security consultants to form a vision for business success. In every case, the process moved the company away from technology and created a safe place to look at applications, assets and liability.

Case Study

A few years ago, I was brought in as the senior manager on an initially small security project. I agreed to work on this project on one condition, that the asset owners be there. After all, policy can't change without stakeholders involved.

Addressing executive management, I asked the first question: "What are you trying to protect?" The data owner began to talk about applications and data. Sometimes it's difficult for the IT representatives to sit through a non-technical discussion, but in the end it helps everyone focus on the things that really matter. Once the problems are defined, technology can be used to help reduce the risk of data loss, misuse or theft.

I gained a clear understanding of what was really important about this project. I knew the systems, understood the importance of the company's brand and its dependence on trust, and I had a feel for the data's sensitivity, confidentiality, integrity and availability.

From there, we talked about relevant threats and the data owner's comfort level. I learned access control and availability were the primary considerations, which isn't uncommon with many projects I've been involved in. I now had a picture that described the data owner's impact versus likelihood graph—the company's risk model.

It turned out, as it often does, that the firewall was not the major requirement for a safe computing environment, but merely a supporting element of security at the perimeter. We spent the rest of the meeting talking about business continuity, access control, identity management, and user awareness. We were able to resolve the root problems in the system.

Most of this company's risk was actually addressed through awareness and policy, while technology played a key role in enforcing the concepts recommended by the team.

The lesson here is simple: ask the question, "What are we trying to protect?" Move the meeting from product to assets, and involve data owners as required to move the project forward.

Competing Product Strategies

If you're working on a project that requires building a security strategy, you'll likely work with or at least understand a number of products that overlap. If you work with manufacturers of security products, you may have been sold various security products that address or incorporate security technology. You may have also engaged smaller boutique security companies to help assess or measure risk. Each has a distinct strategy and will work to gain buy-in at different organizational levels. It's helpful to understand these strategies as you identify assets and build justification for investing in security.

The main issue is to avoid the complexity of integrating incompatible technologies, or to think this is a technical problem.

Companies That Sell Security

As I flip through a copy of *SC Magazine,* I see ads from hundreds of security product companies, which can be broken down into three basic types:

Small, niche security product companies, with only one or two products to sell: These companies are often started by entrepreneurs with a technical bent. The individuals once worked for larger companies, had a great idea, and realized their only way to make money was to get out and start a new company. At some point, they hope to sell the company to a larger one, similar to the one they left.

They sell their solutions based on issues that haven't been addressed in similar product offerings so far. Or they may have a completely new angle that was not addressed, so they have set out to create it. If they can get the attention of the larger companies, they will sell out. Depending on which larger companies you are partnered with, this may be good or bad. If they sell to a network company that is different than your standard, you may find that future releases are customized to larger infrastructure systems that you are not using.

Larger security-only companies. Companies like Symantec, McAfee, Trend Micro, Check Point Software and SonicWall fall into this category. They believe there's a long-term opportunity in the security market and are buying up technologies to create an end-to-end solution around security. They're securing networks and systems, and in some cases provide managed services around security. Their strategy consists of getting larger clients to buy into the overall data protection strategy they provide.

Most of these companies will support any of the major OS or network companies. It's part of their life-blood, so generally this is a safe bet. One word of caution is don't buy on features alone since these companies leap-frog each other year after year. The question generally comes down to who is going to give you the best support and upgrade path. Whatever feature you buy into will change within the next twelve months.

Corporate giants. Companies like Microsoft, Cisco and EMC believe security should be built right into their products. If they're building VoIP technology, they don't go to a third party to secure it. They use built-in security and perhaps upgrade to stronger built-in security features. This goes against the second group of manufacturers, but these companies are buying the first group (the small technology companies). This is also a safe bet if you have invested in infrastructure that has vision and financial stability.

Understanding the Vendor Security Strategy

A few years ago, Network Associates provided clients with a line of products that seemed to have no connection. Network analyzers, help desk software, antivirus, encryption and other offerings in a single portfolio that gave buyers end-user tools, enterprise management, mid-market call centers and home user security. In 2004, the company began transforming itself, renaming products under the McAfee brand.

With management changes, the company divested of Magic, Sniffer and other products that didn't seem to fit. The new company began focusing on security, with acquisitions of Entercept intrusion prevention, Foundstone Enterprise scanning and a number of other technologies, giving McAfee a full suite of security offerings. McAfee developed offerings for the enterprise, with clients like Cisco Systems, the mid-market, SMB and even home users. Its stock went up 40 percent, and execs began to aggressively reengineer their channel.

EMC did the same thing when it added RSA and Network Intelligence to its portfolio, along with tools for virtualization and email archival. With the tools to store and back up data, it added security tools for monitoring and access control to drive a stronger security value proposition. EMC went from being a software company to a business continuity company and, finally, a full security company in 2006. Today they partner with companies that provide identity management software and other asset security tools to provide a safe storage repository for a company's most prized assets.

BMC Software followed suit after picking up Remedy and Magic from Network Associates. With the information technology infrastructure library (ITIL) gaining importance and the announcement of ISO 20000, business services management and security merged. Identity management, change control and the role of the configuration management database (CMDB) in business continuity gave the company a security story and added to BMC's growing list of "Routes to Value" (a security value proposition).

Finally, there's Cisco. In the mid 90s Cisco announced security as a focus area and, since that announcement, has picked up numerous security companies to create a compelling portfolio of security products.

A few years later, I found myself running a national security practice for a global integrator. As a Cisco partner, I was invited to its security VAR council. All of us were struggling to understand where network security products fit in, and were waiting to hear where this company was going to take us. Cisco's strategy was clear: It was building security into the network—a strategy that would provide a new level of security at the network level. Microsoft is now working on similar things on the operating systems side to bundle their anti-virus software into the operating system purchase.

The trends are evident: Security will be part of the infrastructure and part of an overall security strategy. Security point products may lose favor over time with their complexity and integration challenges even if they actually provide greater security benefits at times. With this in mind, it's important that your company consider the best long term strategy, keeping in mind operational costs, technology developments, R&D budgets and efforts, and long term viability of the technology direction you invest in. Expect to combine two or three major strategies to get the full program working.

System Integrator Business Models

Just as there's a complex offering of security technologies, there are also many partners they sell through. It makes sense to know where the best security expertise is going to be found. In general, consulting companies have been weak in their ability to sell high-end security solutions, but more are ramping up to the task as they see its importance. Make sure you are partnering with a company that really understands risk. The benefit here is that integrators can provide expertise along with the product set where larger manufacturers may not.

Let's look at some of the models and providers.

Product Versus Services

Before diving into types of resellers, it's helpful to classify organizations on a continuum—from pure product to visionary consulting.

Product	Resources	Projects	Strategy	Vision

The idea is to get a sense of where organizations really specialize. Are they primarily a commodity product reseller? If so, they may have the best prices simply because they deal in large volume, but their security expertise may not be as strong. In this case, they would fall in the middle or slightly left of the diagram above. If your company is large enough to staff high-end expertise, this may be a good option, however be careful because security is highly specialized when talking about complex operations, so having an expert on call is often worth the cost.

A visionary company helps organizations explore where they're headed, where profitability exists and how to create the direction to get there. This falls to the extreme right. These companies operate at the senior management level and have award winning project management, write great documents, and offer deep discounts because they drive mass quantities of product with little regard for the gross profit made on the sale. Their money comes from pure consulting at the strategic and visionary level. My experience is that they may have a team of security people, but aren't often very strong when it comes to actually implementing security technology.

Companies that fall between these two classifications include staff augmentation or resources provided to existing project teams or operations functions. The "Projects" group would include companies that focus largely on fixed-start and end initiatives, owning the overall scope, development, design, testing and turnover.

"Strategy" focused operations may help companies develop their methodology, process and workflow. My company would most likely fall between Strategy and Vision, as I work with organizations to develop awareness in the area of security, but not actual product implementation or even assessment services.

If I look primarily at the reseller population, most companies fall somewhere between resource and project. Most are working toward more projects, but actually selling more product-install business. Everyone realizes that there is more profit to make when delivering the entire solution, but often the resources to do this are lacking or cost too much.

Security is best delivered by a strong project company. It starts with assessments that measure the risk, and then a road map can be constructed and used to deliver relevant solutions, implementing the right level of security based on your data requirements. Wherever there's a project initiative with a goal of providing greater functionality, operational efficiency or enhanced profitability, risk should be a consideration. If a third party contracted integrator is doing the work, make sure someone understands the security part of the equation.

In the following subsections, I have taken the classic VAR model and created several subcategories to further define your options.

SMB VARs

Smaller VARs buy through distribution and generally treat security as a product sale. Their clients are mostly SMB companies with less than 50 users, with limited needs or ability to buy complex security technologies. Most of these solutions providers have relegated themselves to break/fix work, network fileserver resales and small networking projects. The majority of revenue comes from PC hardware and repair work. More are realizing the threats that are present in the small business space, so look for a company that has made this transition.

If you work in a small to midsized company, don't be fooled into thinking that your company doesn't have security needs just because your solution provider doesn't focus on it. There is a big security concern out there for companies of your size. If not appropriately addressed, it could put you out of business. One option offered by these companies is a remotely managed security service.

When I refer to "security," I mean system availability, data integrity and the ability to restore quickly. If your company is small, you likely lack proper IT staffing and support. I am seeing many untrained companies providing services such as a quarterly "port scan" which comes back with a "green light." This is not a valid test and it's likely that your technology provider is missing the boat. Find a new provider.

Some small integrators have put together their own offering using appliances specifically built to monitor and manage devices on your internal network. When done properly, this can be a good and cost effective solution.

In other cases, large manufacturers such as Cisco, Securview or distributors like Ingram Micro have done the heavy lifting by building out the network operations center, and then are offering a rebranded service through their partner. This in turn gets sold to you and can also be a strong offering, as these larger companies have money to invest in the right back end infrastructure. The local technology provider then monitors the systems, providing the local response arm. It's also a valid and cost effective model.

The measure of competency comes in the company's people that actually show up if there is a problem. Check SLAs, make sure their people are actually available in the moment of a crisis and not out on other jobs, waiting to be pulled off of their engagement. Make sure the model offers after hours support.

Should you go with a larger supplier to ensure a more stable offering? Not necessarily. It's been shown over and over that larger companies have too much overhead to effectively deal with smaller enterprises. When they do, they are stepping down from what they really want to be doing. It's likely that you will not receive the attention you really need and will pay more for services, even if the product comes at a better discount. If you must, mail-order your product and stick with the smaller reseller for the best support, but make sure they actually understand security first.

Mid-Size VARs

The mid-size reseller generally comes out of the Small Business market but has moved up over time, adding expertise in specialized areas. The litmus test is whether or not they actually staff consultants, or just engineers.

Managed security offerings may exist with these companies; however, a different level of support will exist, built for larger and more complex organizations. If you work for a mid-sized company you probably won't get the attention you want from a large manufacturer, so this is a good place to go for expertise and attention.

You should be looking for a supplier that has deep expertise that you can call on. Your IT organization should be involved both to learn more about new and complex technology as well as gaining some insight about what will be required of them after an initiative moves to operations.

Mid-market companies generally won't want to spend the money for high-end security expertise, so it's best to look for it in a partner. This is where the mid-market focused VAR comes into play. Find a midsize supplier that specializes in your size business and perhaps has some level of vertical expertise. The mid-sized match assures you that you'll receive the attention you need. It may be tempting to delegate all security to the technical team, but the likelihood of retaining someone on the IT staff long term with high-end security expertise is small. They will have too many job offers to keep them focused.

The limiting factor comes in your integrator's willingness to train and invest in higher-end resources with consulting capabilities and business acumen. You are going to need this to roll out the appropriate levels of security and end-user awareness training. Focus on this when interviewing possible candidates.

Large Integrators

They might not all be global, but I'm referring to the larger resellers that generally span multiple geographies. These resellers typically sell everything from enterprise storage to mid-range systems, larger network deployments and perhaps applications.

This group generally works with larger organizations as their overhead is high and they staff higher end talent. When dealing with large integrators, be aware of a few things: They tend to deal in large roll-outs and are buying huge quantities of products, bringing the prices down. This could be good for larger companies looking for product at better prices. However, the services side of the business is a big consideration when dealing with security or projects that must consider security – which includes all projects dealing with mission critical assets.

These companies are willing to hire specialized security consultants. Great security consultants often demand higher pay so it takes a company with an understanding of security to be willing to staff this team. Some companies on the other hand will skimp on security talent, favoring generalists in the networking group to carry out specialized assignments like security assessment work. The result should be apparent: The assessment becomes a list of network vulnerabilities for technical eyes only. They don't really understand the process needed for measuring risk to the corporation. As a result, your executive team never gets the information you really need to make wise decisions about asset protection. Remediation projects never materialize, and people wonder why security is not properly implemented.

The solution: Hire companies that have strong consulting skills, security experience and have an interest in the bigger security picture. Look for companies that understand business continuity, security assessments and risk analysis, and may even offer a security managed services solution if you don't plan to build one internally. Having a special group within their organization is a good sign.

Security Boutiques

I am convinced security boutiques exist because of the issues raised in the last section—primarily pay. I can think of at least five companies started by people who once worked for larger integrators in my town, where the larger company was unwilling to meet their salary requirements. They left to form new companies focused solely on security.

These companies tend to do well because there's a need for people who understand the value of assets, the risk associated with today's corporate computing environments and companies' needs to extend their enterprise into new places. They are good at demonstrating value and showing their clients how to defend against today's cyber-criminals, and they are delivering value to the data owner. In every case, this is a recipe for success.

Other larger resellers can duplicate this within their existing business structure if they take the appropriate steps and are willing to look at the bigger picture. The downside to these boutique companies is that they may not really understand some of the infrastructure systems they are working to secure. If you use this type of company, make sure they really possess the knowledge needed to secure areas you are working in such as wireless networking, unified communications, web applications and more. A security person without proper understanding of these supporting technologies may not be able to provide the asset protection needed on a given system.

In general these companies will be high-end and will cost more. They are a good choice in the mid to large companies, and should be part of the larger initiative, not completely isolated from the business.

Managed Services Companies

The last group is fairly new, as they're solution providers who primarily offer their solution as a fully managed service, providing everything you need for security from a central Security Operations Center.

Many technology companies have bought into the idea that managed services is the best way to deliver security. Yet many of these companies are not succeeding. Why?

There are several reasons. First, they may not really understand security. They may have come out of a systems or network background to offer more of a monitoring service but not necessarily true security. There is little value in monitoring just for the sake of monitoring. As an asset owner, you are looking for risk reduction. Somehow, these companies must measure need and then demonstrate a reduction in risk.

Secondly, if a company is going to completely outsource security, you have to know them. There must be a level of trust. If they haven't performed project work for you, how can you trust them with taking over your security? You can't.

The Foundation of a Winning Security Provider

Regardless of whether you buy from a solution provider, reseller or a manufacturer, there are certain principles that make a winning choice.

Focus on Assets, Not Products. Asset-level conversations directly address the needs of your company. Any other approach is going to make security a technology and product decision that will ultimately fail to deliver the security your company needs.

Silo Versus Integrated. Assets must be considered along with the systems that create and support them – you are addressing a business need, not a technology need. This is where assets are created and used, and where liability exists. Consider security as part of every system your company uses to run its business.

It's that asset mindset vs. the technology mindset: a technology mindset uses a silo approach, always looking for a new appliance to purchase The asset mindset thinks in terms of integrated systems.

Security Built in is Best: Treating security issues after the application has been installed is often too late. Think in terms of designing security into the application. If you already have the application, you will have to go back, but consider ways to do this in conjunction with upgrades and redesigns. Bolted on security often fails.

IT Generalists versus Security Specialists. Even though a silo approach is discouraged, you still need experts to understand the risk. This is where outside consultants may make sense. Consider the need for having an advisor that really understands security before implementing. In fact, this person should be brought in as early as possible whenever building out new applications.

As part of any larger initiative, I recommend partnering with an outside consultant or firm that really does understand security, involving your IT organization along with the specialized expertise you don't have in-house, and making this part of the overall business initiative.

Select your partners carefully. You have an overall initiative to secure data throughout the organization, and inside this you have an effort to build the asset mindset into all initiatives that involve computers and data. You should be able to pick what works best for your company size and complexity now that you understand the different strategies used by manufactures and independent software developers, along with the different types of solutions providers and consultants.

Chapter 15

Making Sense of Security

Technology countermeasures cost money. Building response teams takes time away from valuable resources both within the IT department as well as at the departmental level. Staying up on security trends takes time and energy, and of course putting security controls in place often places restrictions on business practices.

Security can make life a little more cumbersome.

In every case, trade-offs between security and functionality must be considered. But with wise choices, we can turn some of the tide coming against us right now with the exponential growth in information theft and cybercrime. It's time to build a new mindset about digital asset security.

The Reality of Attacks

Recent reports indicate that around 70% of all companies report some form of attack and at least half of these involve a level of data theft. Many will involve insiders, and many of these attacks will hit small companies as well as individuals who lack strong security controls.

Automated attacks pose a great risk to everyone these days. These types of attacks have an advantage because we probably won't notice the criminal act and it won't be easy to track down the perpetrator.

Companies that should be concerned about targeted attacks include certain government organizations that deal with sensitive information, large financial institutions, and those that are considered industry leaders in their vertical market. Smaller companies should be on the alert for insiders that will figure out how to make money by working a system they have come to know. New laws are coming that will increase the penalties for accessing confidential information, making it easier for companies to take action when this does happen, but that won't stop the damage. Everyone needs to be on the alert for automated attacks that threaten to add your systems to the growing number of bot nets, or that automatically skim information such as credit card numbers and other information that can be sold for a profit online.

Let law enforcement and specialized government organizations worry about stopping terrorism and cyberwarfare. Your job is to make sure your company is protected with reasonable business continuity and disaster recovery plans, and with technology and policies that will help thwart information misuse and theft.

Reasonable Security Measures

Reasonable security measures or adding a measure of "Due Care" simply means taking reasonable steps to secure the assets under your domain. It's up to asset owners to make wise decisions by asking the three questions: What are you really trying to protect? What are the relevant risks? And how comfortable do you feel with your organization's ability to detect and respond before data is stolen, misused or compromised in some way?

Security is an iterative process. When companies try to implement a solid security program all at once, it rarely meets the need. Restrictions are put in place that keep people from doing their work while the actual levels of risk are not reduced. Assets are not considered and technology becomes the predominant risk mitigation strategy with little in the way of proper policies or training among departments.

Once the security program is built, people have a false sense of security as developments and new frontiers are constantly discovered on the enemy side. An iterative mindset is one of growing and evolving a culture of awareness and safe handling of data. This comes with education across the entire enterprise and some level of enforcement with those using data. Firewalls provide a good example. People still believe they are safe because they have a stateful inspection firewall in place. Nothing could be further from the truth. Another false sense of security comes with the advancements made in anti-virus software. We are not seeing many viruses so therefore we are safe. Again, this is a wrong mindset.

Build your program knowing what will be acceptable to the business and what will be supported by senior managers. Constantly learn about what the relevant threats are to avoid unnecessary restrictions. Always be aware of what you are trading in terms of cost, access and personal freedom. And remember, don't give into the temptation to make this a technical issue. Frequently we see security measures taken that actually create bigger problems or restrictions for the business. One example is banning laptops, as someone wanted to do after the attacks on 9/11. Can you imagine business travel without PDAs and laptops? The same is true when companies suddenly don't allow any instant messaging, PDA tools, or internet access.

Rather than reacting without thinking, proper analysis should be followed as described in the Response Mindset Chapter. This allows the right people to get involved in assessing the relevant threats and building security around the assets that matter. Using a detection response mindset, security is built not to keep everything out, but rather to detect a problem. It's much like a house that requires doors and windows to make it usable.

One more note here, one solution never fits everyone. Each company has different types of asset, different requirements for travel and user access and different political and geographical challenges. The mindset of building the discipline in a way that meets the need of your company is the only way this will work.

Security That Works

Security that works requires asset owners that understand the value of the assets they deal with and their associated liability. Asset owners that leave security to the IT group find their departments submitting to a set of business inhibiting requirements. In the end, these managers are supporting end-users as they look for ways around security measures in an effort to do their job. This creates bad security.

Good security is built when asset owners help IT come up with the best solutions by listening to their insights on relevant threats and working through the realities of what the business requires. Politics always get in the way of helpful discussions such as this, so check your titles at the door.

Don't accept the idea that security is too complex and has to be riddled with technology concepts, three letter acronyms, and discussions of protocol stacks and data packets. Security people can tend to get too technical, making this confusing. It happens in every discipline as we all have our own vernacular, but insist that technical people speak in layman's terms.

The bottom line to good security involves knowing the value of your assets, and who wants access. This is a business issue.

Consider safeguards, but work through the complexities imposed on the business and the people. Be less concerned about creating complex esoteric security strategies, and focus on strong education, simple tools, and effective execution when handling and safeguarding assets. Create a mindset that is open to audits like we have in accounting. Proper audits make sense, and constant assessing is essential to good security.

All large companies have politics and agendas. Understanding what people need personally may help you weed through why certain things are allowed and others are not, and why certain technology choices are made verses others.

Can you build a bullet proof security program? It's always the wrong question. Stop asking this question and stop accepting the answer, "We've got it covered." No one has it covered, and no organization is very well protected. Rather go back to the mindsets.

1. Learn about the assets from an asset owner standpoint.

2. Have a restrictive mindset, knowing that authorized users of data really do need access and need to be equipped and able to do their work.

3. Make sure you understand digital assets. They're invisible, ubiquitous, accessible but hard to delete. Become digitally aware.

4. Be alert and don't feel that false sense of security as IT takes on the task of information security.

5. Be ready to respond, knowing that malicious code does get in, and most companies are hit with some form of security violation, many of which involve insiders.

6. Continue to assess and audit, looking for weaknesses in the system or violations and misuse of the system

7. Iteratively build out a holistic security program, filling in all nine boxes, driven by asset owners across the company, but managed centrally.

You can't ensure complete safety, but Protection, Detection and Response go a long way in keeping people from testing the system. When they do, the alarm will sound, the well rehearsed response will go into action, and your assets will be secured before real damage is done. That's what real security is about.

Dave Stelzl

LaVergne, TN USA
23 March 2010
176828LV00004B/1/P